100 WAYS
TO BUILD
TEAMS

By

Carol Scearce

IRI/Skylight Training and Publishing
Palatine, IL

100 Ways to Build Teams
Fifth Printing

Published by IRI/Skylight Training and Publishing, Inc.
200 East Wood Street, Suite 274
Palatine, IL 60067
800-348-4474, 847-991-6300
FAX 847-991-6420
irisky@xnet.com
http://www.business1.com/iri_sky/

Creative Director: Robin Fogarty
Editors: Julia E. Noblitt, Erica Pochis
Book Designer: Bruce Leckie
Cover Designer: David Stockman
Manuscript Preparer: Donna Ramirez
Production Coordinator: John Conick

Library of Congress Catalog Card Number 92-62450

Printed in the United States of America.
ISBN 0-932935-47-8

1130D-2-96V
Item number 0881

CONTENTS

ESTABLISHING ROLES AND RESPONSIBILITIES 63

CODE OF CONDUCT 89

ACKNOWLEDGMENTS

M y acknowledgments are kind of like the academy awards. I have so many people to thank.

My first thanks go to Robin Fogarty. I remember saying to Robin, "If I do this and it is awful you better not tell anyone I wrote a book we had to throw away." Robin, thanks most of all for your belief in me. I could not have done this without your encouragement.

Thanks to my editor, Julie Noblitt, who was so kind. Julie you should be a PR agent. You were so gentle with your suggestions.

To Bruce Leckie, who did the layout for this book, a thousand thanks. You are a miracle worker. I find myself looking at the book and saying, "I can't believe it's the real thing!" You made it so inviting.

A big hug to my husband, David O'Brien, who knew when to talk to me and when not to. I love you.

I must say thanks to Larry Lezotte who gave me my first big break with teaming. Larry, my life in North Carolina has never been the same. Thanks for the invitation.

Thank you Lydia McCue, who worked with Larry Lezotte, and vouched for me. You also gave me a great start in West Virginia with teaming.

Thanks to all the educators across the country who helped me try out all these activities over the years. You did them so well and with such gusto. It is because of you that I have such wonderful stories. I admire your courage in trying to change the system.

Many thanks to my neighbors, Herb, Marlene, and Tracy who encouraged me on a daily basis. I'll remember the times in your kitchen when all of you teased me about going on the Today Show with autographed copies. I think we might have to wait a while for that one.

Last but not least, I must thank my old faithful companion, SugarBear. You laid under the computer listening to a lot of strange noises coming from the computer and my mouth. You never barked once when I missed your afternoon walks.

FOREWORD

If leaders are to succeed in changing the entrenched culture of their organizations, they must have a strategy for planned change. The leaders must take into account the need for changing both the norms, beliefs, or policies and procedures of the organization. In addition, and at least as important, the leaders need a strategy that will change the way people in that organization behave. Virtually all successful change reduces itself to people change—no small undertaking!

What tools do the leaders have available to create the conditions that will assure behavioral change in the people who make up an organization? Essentially, the tools that can be used are limited indeed. Some leaders depend heavily on "stick power" to change people. They believe that intimidation, and the threat of punishment will produce sustained, positive behavioral change. Evidence that stick power is effective is, at best, overstated. Some leaders believe that sustained, positive behavioral change can be achieved by carefully deploying "carrot power"—that if you can create the appropriate rewards and incentives, the desired behavior can be solicited and maintained. The payoff from the careful use of carrot power is a little more positive. But if the carrot power tool is to be used effectively, three conditions must exist. First, the leaders must have an inexhaustible supply of carrots; second, the workers must have an insatiable appetite for carrots; and third, and most important, both the leaders and workers must know precisely what behavior will yield the carrots—no small undertaking!

More enlightened leaders have come to realize that the best hope for creating positive, sustained behavioral change in an organization occurs when the tool of "hug power" is used. According to the noted economist and author, Kenneth Boulding, hug power is the power that comes when two or more people connect with each other because of shared beliefs, vision, and values. The resulting synergy represents a very powerful force for sustained positive change. Unfortunately, to unleash the force of hug power means that the people must have the time and opportunity to develop the openness and trust required to discuss beliefs, vision, and values authentically—no small undertaking!

The development of a plan to tap the potential hug power in an organization must start with creating teams of individuals who are willing to risk the openness and trust that is required. Carol Scearce's book represents a valuable source of proven methods and procedures for building effective work teams. These techniques should not be seen as ends in themselves. Rather these proven practices, as well as the creation of work teams, represent the one best tool we have for changing today's workplace so that it will better serve our society and the society our children will inherit—no small undertaking!

Lawrence W. Lezotte

INTRODUCTION

E ach year I get many calls from organizations across the country
asking for help in establishing teams. I refer them to many excellent
sources including videos, books, and audiotapes. It is not long before
they call back saying, "The sources are great but we have a few problems. First of all we don't have time to read all the books. Second, we
don't really know how to transfer the information to real life." So, I find
myself packing my suitcase and traveling thousands of miles to offer
assistance.

As I reflect on my journeys to these organizations, I find that most of
them cannot afford the number of consulting days that it takes to institute quality team building. Their main problem is not in understanding what they read but in how to process the information. I can't tell you
how many times someone says to me, "Carol, if we just had something
that would be fun to use and help us process role clarification, how to
select a leader, how to celebrate our successes, or any of the other topics
you have mentioned we could do it on our own."

I pondered the problem and decided that maybe an easy-to-use recipe
book on the essential areas of teaming would be the answer. That's how
100 Ways to Build Teams was born. I would like to make two points
clear: This is not a book on the theories of teaming. There are many
excellent books that cover this adequately. I have listed them for you in
the bibliography. This book does not cover all aspects of teaming; it
covers the essential components of teaming. If these components are not
included in team development the team will not function.

I feel compelled to mention that two important areas not included in
this book are problem solving and conflict management. My rationale for
leaving them out is that an attempt to cover them in a chapter would be

an injustice. However, in the chapters on Code of Conduct and Managing Meetings I have activities that include a way to learn about these two areas if the team is willing to invest the time. As an experienced team player let me say that it is worth the price you pay in time.

WHO SHOULD USE THIS BOOK?

One of the nice things about this book is that it can be used by anyone who works with people.

- Teachers can use it in cooperative learning.
- Principals can use it for faculty meetings.
- Students can use it for clubs and organizations.
- Superintendents can use it for school boards and other meetings.
- Businesses can use it for meetings.
- Professional organizations can use it for meetings.
- Any type of work team can use it to establish teams.

All you need to do is pick up this book and let it work for you.

WHAT IS THE BEST WAY TO USE THIS BOOK?

I would like to invite you to walk through the different sections with me so that you will become familiar with the book.

INTRODUCTION

Each chapter is preceded by a short introduction that explains why the chapter is important. Sometimes I have included stories or examples from my own or others' personal experiences that enhance the meaning of the topic. Feel free to use these stories in your own team training. At times there is additional information that might help you if someone asks you a question or wants to know more about the topic.

QUOTATIONS

Each section has a quotation that captures the essence of the chapter. I have found that quotations have a way of awakening the brain. People love them, and often the quotation is so powerful that you can hear people sigh. It's almost as if they are saying, "Ah, yes, now I understand." My suggestion is that you use the quotation as your opening line to the study of the topic.

BACKGROUND

Each section begins with a true story about the topic. If you use humor and stories, you can effectively and easily introduce a topic, make important points, and touch on sensitive issues.

One of my stories may spark a memory of something that happened to you that you could share. The key point here is that from the beginning of time stories have been used to convey powerful messages. Use them!

DID YOU KNOW

This section is a list of some important points that the team needs to know. All points come from resources I have collected over the years. I wish they were all original but they are not. They are a collection from the best minds across the world on teaming.

It is from this section that you can develop a mini lecture. If you would like to develop a longer lecture I suggest that you look under the DID YOU KNOW sections for all three levels of the topic. For example, each chapter has three levels: *Simple Things to Do, Things That Take Effort,* and *For the Committed.* Each level has more facts. You can take all three levels and put together an extensive lecture.

SIMPLE THINGS TO DO

Each topic begins with activities that are simple. This level is designed for teams who are in the "forming" stage. This stage is characterized by excitement, optimism, pride, suspicion, fear, and anxiety. During this stage there is not a high level of trust. Team members don't do business any differently than before. *Simple Things to Do* will get a team started. If you do not have a lot of time this is the section for you.

THINGS THAT TAKE EFFORT

This level is designed to help team members move through the "storming" stage which is characterized by arguing among members, defensiveness and competition, establishing unrealistic goals, and concern about excessive work. During this stage members realize something is not right. They aren't really collaborating and functioning as a team. They are beginning to realize that teaming takes effort. This level is for teams who have some time to spend learning about teaming.

FOR THE COMMITTED

This level is designed to help team members move to the "norming" and "performing" stages. In the norming stage the team has realized that teaming as a way of doing business takes a lot of work. They accept teaming as a way to do things and believe that everything is going to work out. They attempt to gain harmony, they are friendlier, they confide in each other, they share problems, and they have a sense of team cohesion, common spirit, and goals. They are ready to establish and maintain norms. With commitment and hard work they will move to the performing stage which is characterized by a better understanding of group processes, better understanding of others' strengths and weaknesses, a high level of trust, and satisfaction at the team's progress. They work through problems and have formed a close attachment to the team.

It is up to your team to decide where they want to begin. My suggestion is to look through the activities on all the levels and select the ones that best suit your team's needs. It could be that you are on one level for one topic and another level for another topic. The beauty of this book is that you can mix and match to suit your needs.

MATERIALS YOU WILL NEED

After each activity the materials you will need are listed. I have seen many an activity fail because the team did not have the materials. Resources are sometimes limited, so I have tried to suggest materials that organizations already have. Most of the activities can be done using only chart paper, magic markers, and masking tape. Please feel free to add any materials you think will make the activity better. There will always be a sample in the directions or an illustration of the handout.

BIBLIOGRAPHY

The bibliography is not extensive but the sources listed are excellent. You can get them in most book stores.

That completes our tour of the book. I hope you found it helpful. Do not limit your potential by using the book only as I have suggested. It is my hope that you will find *100 Ways to Build Teams* user-friendly and that it will make your journey into teaming fun, exciting, and successful. Have fun! Teaming is the right thing to do.

TRUST
BUILDING

One Saturday morning, when I was a teenager, a group of friends and I went to Goofy Falls, a beautiful body of water in the interior of Panama. It was during the rainy season, but on this day there was no sign of rain. In fact, the forecast was great! After a morning and afternoon of swimming I grew tired and decided to take one more jump off the top of the falls. I took my jump and then sat on the rocks below to watch everyone. Suddenly I heard a loud roar. I looked up and saw people at the top of the falls running. Someone yelled, "Get out of the water!" Just as I started to get up I looked up and saw a wall of water coming over the top of the falls at breakneck speed. I was not fast enough. I was swept away in something we had often heard about but never experienced...a dreaded mountain flash flood. The water took me miles down the river, over rocks, under trees, you name it, I think I went over it. For some reason the water threw me up on a fallen tree. I was able to grab hold. I pulled myself out of the flood waters and sat shaking and scared to death.

After what seemed like an eternity I heard a voice. I looked up and standing in the jungle was a young G. I. with his hand out beckoning for me to come with him. I had no idea who he was but something about his face, his eyes, and his voice told me it was okay. It took quite a while to make our way back. Even then we had to be rescued. We were on the wrong side of the falls. The rescue team secured a rope across the rushing water and told me to hang on so they could help me across. I would not budge. Not me! The water was too swift. I felt a hand on my shoulder and heard a voice say, "I'll tie you on my back and carry you across the rope myself." It was the young G. I. I immediately stopped crying and did as he said. The onlookers cheered as we safely reached the other side. Why, when I was almost in shock, did I follow someone I didn't know?

I was too young at the time to understand but as I reflect back on the young man I now realize that he radiated confidence when he spoke. His body and his message were congruent. He had to have had integrity to jump into a flash flood to save someone he didn't know, and he was certainly reliable. These are some of the characteristics of trust.

That's what this chapter is all about. I purposely placed it first in the book because of its importance to the success of the team. Without trust the team will stay in the "storming" stage —characterized by difficulties, conflicts, unhealthy confrontation, etc. Without trust the team will not move to the performing stage which is essential in order for the team to do its job.

Dr. Edwards Deming's Fourteen Points of Management talk about breaking down barriers between departments. He suggests putting everybody to work to accomplish the transformation of an organization. Teaming is one of the vehicles he suggests to put everyone to work. He talks about the fact that everyone has something to contribute. Without trust team members will not work together; the team will eventually wither and die.

I recommend that teams begin every meeting with a trust-building activity. When teams are first forming they need to devote fifteen minutes of the first ten meetings to trust building. As they move to the "norming" stage (characterized by an attempt to achieve harmony, friendliness, a sense of team cohesion, and establishing team ground rules) and the "performing" stage (characterized by constructive self-change, close attachment to the team, and high productivity), they can cut the trust-building time down to five to ten minutes per meeting.

It is better to suffer wrong than to do it, and happier to be sometimes cheated than not to trust.—Dr. Samuel Johnson

TRUST ME, THE CHECK IS IN THE MAIL

BACKGROUND

I find that people are full of uninformed optimism when they first work together. They want to skip the trust-building section and get on to the task at hand. To do so is a big mistake. While designing a program for a middle school I asked the principal how much work the staff needed to do to build trust. He assured me that the members of his staff cared for each other, worked well together, and were ready for the high-level teaming skills. "Skip the touchy-feely stuff!" he said. I did and I must tell you it was the worst training day of my life. They "niced" each other to death over the roles, they reluctantly shared ideas, and they wouldn't share ideas with other teams. Some didn't talk at all, some actually admitted to me they did not like their team, and two or three kept saying in a small voice, "We're new here...what's going on?" I went back to my hotel room and did what Madeline Hunter calls "monitoring and adjusting." What these teachers needed was the first level of trust building. They needed to start out with simple, non-threatening activities.

DID YOU KNOW

- People use communication barriers such as criticism, name-calling, threatening, and moralizing over ninety percent of the time when dealing with a problem or a need to be fulfilled.
- The most common cause of team failure is the inability of team members to get along...i.e., there's no trust.
- People often think trust is automatically built in to their team because they are committed and have good will.

Simple
Things
To
Do

Trust Talk

Ask each team member to think of a person he or she really trusts. It can be someone in his or her personal or professional life. Allow one minute for each team member to think. Then ask them to share with the group three characteristics the person has that makes him or her trustworthy. Go around the group and ask each person to share his or her characteristics as the recorder writes them on a chart. Then lead the group in a discussion about how the team might use these characteristics to develop trust. As the team makes suggestions the recorder lists them on another piece of chart paper. Tape the list on the wall so the team can refer to the ideas every now and then to see how they are doing.

Trustworthy
1. honest
2. loyal
3. friendly
4.
5.
6.
7.
8.

MATERIALS YOU WILL NEED
2 pieces of chart paper
masking tape
magic markers

Simple
Things
To
Do

#2

You're On

Tell the group that you will ask each team member to talk about himself or herself for three minutes. They may talk about family, profession, hobbies, or anything else that will help the team know them better. Give them a minute to think of what they are going to say. When the minute is up ask everyone to get a piece of paper and a pencil. As each team member shares, any member who has a question jots it down so he or she can ask the person after all the team members have shared. Ask someone to begin. After three minutes, call time and move on to the next person. When everyone has had a turn, open up the floor and allow anyone to ask questions or discuss information they found interesting. When everyone has asked all their questions, ask how this activity has helped team members get to know each other better.

MATERIALS YOU WILL NEED
a piece of paper and a pencil for each team member

Simple
Things
To
Do

Feeling Groovy

A sk each team member to list on a piece of paper three things that could happen so that at the end of the team meetings he or she could walk away and say, "Wow I enjoyed working with my team today. It was great!" Examples might be humor, support for ideas, and being treated with respect. Allow one or two minutes for the team to write, then call on one team member at a time. Ask each member to share his or her thoughts and clarify when needed. The recorder writes the responses on a chart. Tape the chart on the wall and refer to it from time to time to check on how the needs of the group are being met.

THIS MEETING
WAS GREAT!

1.) short
2.) people listened
to each other
3.) we accomplished
one of our
Goals
4.) Donuts

MATERIALS YOU WILL NEED
a piece of paper and a pencil for each team member
1-2 pieces of chart paper
masking tape
a magic marker

T-Shirt Art

Tell the team members they are going to spend some time talking about themselves. Suggestions for sharing are books they like, favorite TV programs, what they like best about their jobs, what motivates them to work, what characteristics they have that will make them a valuable team member, etc. Then give the team a large sheet of chart paper and magic markers. Have them cut a large T-shirt out of the chart paper. Then ask them to design a logo with a slogan on it that represents their team. For example, if they see themselves as caring they could adopt the bear as their logo and have the slogan "Because We Care!" Another team may see themselves as caring and have five sombreros as their symbol with the slogan "Five Amigos Working Toward Transformation."

MATERIALS YOU WILL NEED
chart paper
magic markers
scissors

Simple
Things
To
Do

Business Cards

This activity is a great one to do after the team has met a couple of times and knows each other better. Tell team members that they have spent a great deal of time getting to know and understand each other. Tell them that as a team they are going to design a business card that represents them and what they stand for. They will have it printed and share it with other staff. For example, a team with a "care bear" logo might design a business card with bear paws on it. The card might list the members' names and a sentence that says "Call 1-800-WE-CARE if you need help and support."

MATERIALS YOU WILL NEED
a piece of poster board or chart paper
assorted magic markers
printed business cards

The Name Game

Ask the team members to come up with three self-descriptive words that start with the first letter of their first name. For example, Carol may use the words caring, comical, and committed to describe herself to her team. The recorder writes the descriptors on a chart. Lead the team in a discussion about how these characteristics of team members will make them a powerful team.

MATERIALS YOU WILL NEED
1 piece of chart paper
a magic marker

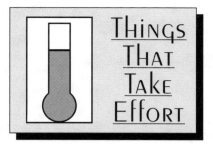

Things That Take Effort

I wish I had some way to make a bridge from man to man...Man is all we've got.—Cross Daman in Richard Wright's *Outsider*

YOU CAN DEPEND ON ME

BACKGROUND

Not long ago I was in New York just beginning a workshop. I had my attention grabber ready. Just as I was about to begin a young man in the workshop walked up and said, "Hi, you and I have a mutual friend." I smiled at him and asked who it was. He then told me something I had told our mutual friend in confidence. When he finished he said, "She told me you wouldn't mind her sharing with me because you were a very open person." I was so stunned and offended. All morning I was very uncomfortable. I ended up having dinner with the young man and lunch the next day. It wasn't until the last day of the workshop that I began to feel comfortable with him. We spent some time getting to know each other during which we established a friendship. We progressed to a new level of trust but I must admit it took some effort. Trust amongst colleagues is very much like that. Trust builds gradually, incrementally, and with effort. As the team matures, the level of trust increases. The members no longer feel a need to hide their feelings. They begin to level with each other and let their guard down. Members believe they can reveal aspects of themselves and their work without fear of being judged by team members.

DID YOU KNOW

- Trust influences all aspects of human interaction.
- Trust will develop over time if the team is moving in positive directions. Trust will increase or decrease depending on how the members react to each other.
- As trust builds members are open to learning from each other.
- Team members who laugh and take risks together build trust at a faster rate and on a higher level than if they do not.

11

Things
That
Take
Effort

Secrets

Ask the members to divulge something they have never told about themselves. An example might be something that happened their first year on the job, or a negative opinion they formed about someone that turned out to be wrong. When everyone has had a turn, tell the team not to be misled into thinking this is an easy activity. It takes quite a bit of trust to reveal mistakes.

MATERIALS YOU WILL NEED

Things
That
Take
Effort

I'll Show You Mine
If You'll Show Me Yours

A sk team members to bring a special artifact to the team meeting. It should be something that is really meaningful to them. For example, one member might bring a picture of his or her grandparents. Another member might bring a baby shoe. They are to explain what it means to them and why it is important. Explain to the team that these things help them get to know each other better. Tell the team that trust is built through sharing parts of ourselves with others.

MATERIALS YOU WILL NEED
artifacts from each person

Things
That
Take
Effort

Trust Creature

Ask the team to share the reasons they trust each other. List attributes of their team that indicate trust on a chart. Tell them that as a team they will create a creature that represents the attributes they listed. Have them hang the Trust Creature in their meeting room. If applicable, have them share their creatures with the other teams.

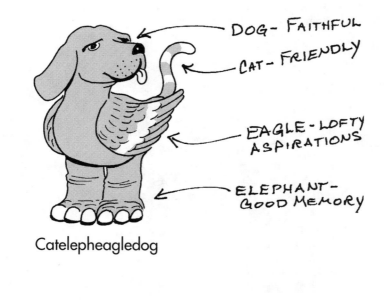

DOG - FAITHFUL

CAT - FRIENDLY

EAGLE - LOFTY ASPIRATIONS

ELEPHANT - GOOD MEMORY

Catelepheagledog

MATERIALS YOU WILL NEED
1 piece of chart paper
construction paper
assorted magic markers
scissors
glue
masking tape

Human Trust Check

Construct a human trust graph on the wall by placing three signs spaced about five feet apart. The signs should read, from left to right, HIGH, MEDIUM, and LOW. Tell each team member to stand under the sign that best represents his or her feelings about the trust level in the group. Ask the resulting groupings to discuss among themselves why they feel the way they do about the trust level of the team. Tell them that after they have a few minutes to discuss, a person they select will share their grouping's thoughts with the whole team. Call the entire team back together and ask each representative to share his or her group's thoughts. Then have the team brainstorm ways to help overcome any low- and medium-level concerns. End the activity by focusing on the high-trust responses.

MATERIALS YOU WILL NEED
3 large cards labeled HIGH, MEDIUM, and LOW
masking tape
3 pieces of chart paper
3 magic markers

Everyone has a vast capacity for being more understanding, respectful, warm, genuine, open, direct, and concrete in his human relationships.
—George Gazda, educator

PEOPLE WHO NEED PEOPLE ARE THE LUCKIEST PEOPLE

BACKGROUND

I was a little nervous as I began the workshop at Townline Elementary school. I had worked with the group before and had planned some sophisticated activities. I gave the first set of directions and watched as the "wild rumpus" began. I was the observer and was to record their behaviors. Words cannot express how these people worked together. I'm not sure I've ever seen a staff like this. They were so open, full of fun, honest, supportive, and at least ten other adjectives. If people made mistakes, it was no big deal and they would try something else. The great thing was that if I hadn't known who the principal was I would not have been able to pick him out of the group during this activity. He was one of them. What was it? What was making this staff appear to be different? It wasn't that they had mastered all the teaming skills. In fact, they had a hard time reaching consensus. It seemed as if they had no written norms of behavior for team work, and they all talked at once. They still had a lot of room for improvement. All of a sudden it dawned on me...they trusted each other. I mean absolutely and completely. They felt totally free to be who they really were. I have to say it was a joy to watch. My nervousness disappeared and when they voted to adopt me I came willingly into the Townline family.

DID YOU KNOW

- The leader of the team must always monitor the level of trust closely, for without trust the team will not continue to function effectively.
- Authenticity is the key element of trust.
- Trust develops from adequate or total information so that individuals can influence or make decisions and control their own work.

For
the
Committed

Burst Write

A sk each team member to write a one-page paper on the importance of trust on a team. Their papers should talk about essential characteristics team members must exhibit, what would cause them not to trust, etc. Tell them to use the "Burst Write" technique wherein they write for five minutes without stopping or editing. Give them one week to complete the paper. At the next team meeting ask the members to share their thoughts. Label three pieces of chart paper as follows: Importance of Trust, Essential Characteristics, and Behaviors That Cause Low Trust. Record what the members share. Lead the team in a discussion of things they can consciously and systematically do to encourage a high level of trust. Together, design a plan that includes activities that reinforce trust.

MATERIALS YOU WILL NEED
a piece of paper and a pencil for each team member
3 pieces of chart paper
masking tape
a magic marker

#12

Wonderful Me

Distribute the "Wonderful Me" handout.

WONDERFUL ME

List 5-6 words that describe you.

What kind of animal best describes you?

What musical instrument best describes you?

What food best describes you?

Animal	Musical Instrument	Food

Tell the team members that as they think about the images they have of themselves, they are to work quickly and record their first thoughts. Once they finish, they go to the boxes at the lower half of the page and interpret the meaning of the words they have used to describe themselves. In other words, if a member described herself as an eagle, she should describe why or how she is like an eagle.

Make a chart using the model below. Have each team member share what they have written on their worksheet. Write down what they say on the chart.

Team Member / Category	1	2	3	4	5
5-6 words					
Animal					
Musical Instrument					
Food					

Discuss what each team member gained or achieved through this activity. Discuss how this process reinforces a high level of trust.

MATERIALS YOU WILL NEED
a copy of the "Wonderful Me" handout for each team member
a large chart for gathering responses
magic markers
masking tape

MISSION
MAKING

Charles Garfield, in his book Peak Performers, *tells the story of a senior vice-president of an aerospace company who couldn't understand the high motivation level of some of his employees. They had such mechanical and repetitive jobs. He acknowledged that the group's job was essential to the success of the plant. In fact if they didn't do their job well it could mean extensive damage to the plant. Garfield's curiosity was piqued. When he visited the department, he noticed that all the workers wore green surgical smocks. "Oh, you noticed," the foreman said. "I got them from my son. He's a cardiovascular surgeon, and he got them so I could give them to the gang. We wear them because we are surgeons, just like my son. He takes care of pipes in the body and we take care of pipes in this plant. It isn't going to have any breakdowns as long as we're working on its arteries." Stenciled on the workers' locker doors was "DR." Their mission statement was "Take care of these pipes the way a doctor takes care of your heart." Their mission motivated them to those high levels of commitment and performance.*

This story illustrates so well the importance of a team's mission. The mission should clearly define what the team cares about and wants to accomplish. It is through the mission that team members become committed. Mission statements empower people and lead them to action. Missions enable teams to concentrate on what is important, collaborate on how they are going to carry out the mission, set quality standards, and communicate what the organization stands for.

21

The mission statement should embody the answers to these questions:

      1. Who will deliver the service?

      2. Who will benefit?

      3. What is the nature of the service?

      4. What constitutes observable evidence?

      5. What is the level of accountability?

The mission becomes a basis of resource allocation, which could be time, money, or people. The team should discuss and evaluate the mission on a regular basis. The mission is the basis of measurable goals and team outcomes. The team may refer to it when important decisions are made. It becomes the driving force of the team.

This chapter is near the beginning of the book because of its importance to the success of team building. The mission should be intact when the team is being formed.

"Vision setting is the domain of leaders."—Monte Moses

UP, UP, AND AWAY

BACKGROUND

"I really don't know why I am here."

"I was told to attend!"

"I was absent the day I was selected."

"Our school voted to go to the teaming concept, that's all I know."

"I'm representing my company's improvement team. We are going to be doing some things together so I'm here to learn how."

Do these statements sound familiar? In most of the workshops I conduct on teaming about three-fourths to one half of the participants don't have a clear picture of their mission. These participants usually want me to tell them what their mission is! I've always wondered why they think *I* would know if *they* don't know. My guess is that because humans are teleological by nature, meaning "we seek out and move toward that which we can picture," we are desperate for a clear mission. In order to be committed to an idea, we have to know what we're being asked to commit to!

DID YOU KNOW

- It is a leader's job to get people thinking along the same lines.
- The leader's role in planning is to share his or her vision and then empower as many people as possible whose contributions will ensure successful planning.
- The leader needs to create a shared image of what the team can become.
- Teams need a vision of greatness that can propel them to unprecedented levels of performance.

23

Simple
Things
To
Do

Keep It Simple

This process for writing a mission is the simplest method. It is quick, and will suffice for some teams. Place a large piece of paper on the wall with the following statement:

The major reasons for the development of this team
are to achieve the following:

Spend some time discussing the reasons with the team and list the responses on a chart. Then ask the team to synthesize its thoughts into three or four sentences. You may want to have them do activity #19 ("Top Five") first to generate a list of values and then see how many of them are represented in the team mission. For example, if one of their shared values is learning from colleagues, they should see that through the teaming effort they will have the opportunity to do so. This may be the first time they have taken the time to talk about what they value! If the team has similar values, then their teaming mission will most likely be successful.

MATERIALS YOU WILL NEED
1 piece of chart paper
a magic marker
masking tape

Let's Get Graphic

G ive each team a large sheet of paper and five magic markers of assorted colors. Tell them to spend fifteen minutes discussing why they are using the teaming approach. They then must represent their thoughts with a graphic organizer, a visual representation of their discussion. An example would be a school that is moving to the middle school concept. Let's say the team discusses things like, many heads are better than one, students become real when all of us focus on them, we can learn from each other, our mission is to serve each student more effectively, etc. The team would then look at all their comments and thoughts and create a picture that symbolizes their discussion. Allow thirty minutes for the team to complete the graphic organizer. If a number of teams are doing this activity then they can share their graphic organizers with each other.

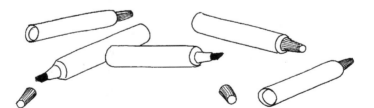

MATERIALS YOU WILL NEED
chart paper
assorted magic markers
masking tape

Simple
Things
To
Do

Let's Use Our Senses

G ive the team a large piece of paper and instruct the members to draw an eye in one column, an ear in the second column, and a heart in the third column.

Ask them to discuss the mission of the team as they perceive it. They are to list concrete behaviors under the three columns, behaviors that would be occurring if everyone understood the mission of the team. Give examples to make sure the team understands the task. For example, you might tell the team that under "Looks Like" they might write "people working collaboratively." Under "Sounds Like" they might write "It is nice not to have to solve all my problems alone." Under "Feels Like" they might write "a sense of belongingness." If a number of teams are doing this activity they might share their charts with other teams.

MATERIALS YOU WILL NEED
chart paper
magic markers
masking tape

Simple
Things
To
Do

A Penny for Your Thoughts

A sk each team member to get out a sheet of paper and be ready to work individually. Tell the team members that you are going to ask them to think about something they are very familiar with, have touched hundreds of times, have thrown away, have wished for, have thought was worthless, and have been counting since they were two years old...a penny. They are to list as many attributes of a penny as they can remember. After about five minutes ask them to get a partner and make a new list. Then, after five minutes they are to get with their entire team and make a master list of at least nineteen attributes. Give each team a penny and let them check their list. When they are finished, lead them in a discussion about what they learned about the team mission from this activity.

MATERIALS YOU WILL NEED
a piece of paper and a pencil per person
a piece of chart paper and a magic marker per team
pennies

Simple
Things
To
Do

What's a Team to Do?

A sk each team member to draw a web on a piece of paper. Use the web model in the illustration below. Have them list words on their individual webs that describe their perception of their team's mission. Allow five minutes for individuals to complete their webs. Then have everyone share their responses and create a new team web that has all of their perceptions on one piece of paper. Then lead them in a discussion about the mission of the team.

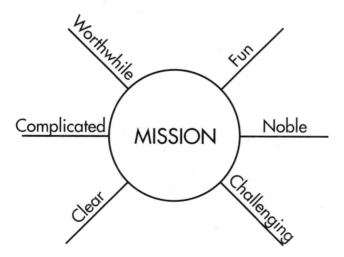

MATERIALS YOU WILL NEED
a piece of paper and a pencil per team member
a piece of chart paper and a magic marker per team

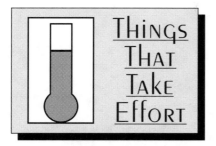

A mission is worthless unless it's put to work.—George Patterson

LET'S DO IT TOGETHER

BACKGROUND

I noticed when I mentioned the word "mission" to a group of educators they groaned. I was curious and asked what the problem was. They admitted they had a mission but that it had been a pain. They said their mission statement was about four or five sentences long. They knew it was O.K. because they had called their colleagues at other schools to compare mission statements. One member said, "Since they all look alike why not have a mission swapping party, take the best from all, and sell it to anyone needing a mission?" That comment brought laughter from the group.

One of the reasons many people don't get excited about drafting a mission statement is that no one has ever taught them the process. Unfortunately, many of us have not been encouraged to take risks. We have not been told that failure is not fatal. No one wants to admit they don't know how to do something. People sometimes suffer through a task just to get it done. There are a number of processes that will help teams develop a mission. Some are more involved than others. The trick is to find the one that best suits your needs and do it. Having a team mission statement is key to the success of a team.

DID YOU KNOW

- To succeed in a big way, a team needs to think as one.
- A mission has to be a team thing. Everyone has to buy into it.
- Every team must have a mission. Without a mission the team will cease to exist.
- Values are basic to all matters of choice and decision.

Things
That
Take
Effort

What Am I Living For?

E xplain to the team members that they will use this activity to discuss
values. Human beings are value-driven; they tend to act on things
they value. Put the following questions on a chart:

> • What do I want out of my professional life?
> • What do I count as personal profit from my job?
> • What do I like about my job?
> • What do I believe about my job?
> • What is my definition of job success?

Ask each team member to take thirty minutes to reflect on responses
to the questions. Have them share answers to come up with how they are
alike and how they are different. Ask them to write for three minutes
(without stopping) about how the values activity relates to their perception of their teaming mission.

MATERIALS YOU WILL NEED
a piece of paper and a pencil for each team member
chart paper
a magic marker

Things
That
Take
Effort

Top Five

T op Five is a good way to discuss values because the examples are there for the team. Give each team member a copy of the following handout:

TOP FIVE

Dedication to student growth

Promoting self-esteem

Belief in evolving abilities

Total development of the student

Dedication to school improvement

Dedication to personal and professional growth

Loyalty to staff and school

Honesty and forthrightness

Cooperative support

Upholding school procedures

Note: If the team is not a school team, modify the Top Five handout to fit the organization. For example, instead of "Dedication to student growth," it may be "Dedication to customer growth." Instead of "Dedication to school improvement" it may be "Dedication to organization or department improvement."

Ask team members to rank order the ten items according to the ones they value the most with 1 being the most valued to 10 the least valued. Ask the team members to share their rankings. Once they have shared, place a card with each value on the wall. Have the team vote on each value using the chart on the next page, and try to reach consensus on the top five values of the team. Lead them in a discussion of the importance of understanding what their teammates value and how it relates to their idea of the team's mission.

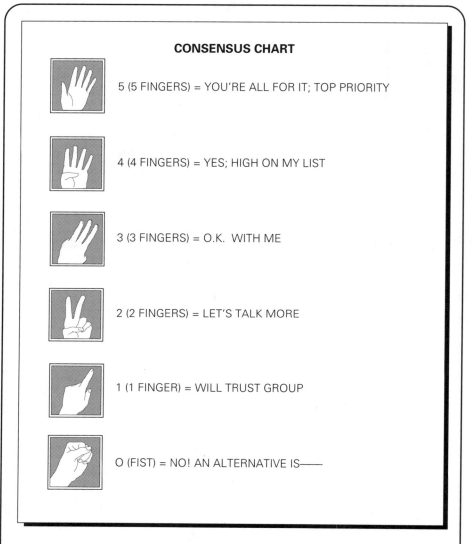

CONSENSUS CHART

5 (5 FINGERS) = YOU'RE ALL FOR IT; TOP PRIORITY

4 (4 FINGERS) = YES; HIGH ON MY LIST

3 (3 FINGERS) = O.K. WITH ME

2 (2 FINGERS) = LET'S TALK MORE

1 (1 FINGER) = WILL TRUST GROUP

O (FIST) = NO! AN ALTERNATIVE IS——

MATERIALS YOU WILL NEED

a copy of the "Top Five" handout and a pencil per person

1 set of large index cards with the values from the "Top Five" handout
written on them

1 enlarged copy of the Consensus Chart

masking tape

Things
That
Take
Effort

Why Are We Here?

I nvite the team to a mission meeting. Set up the room so that no more than six people are sitting at a table. Distribute a piece of chart paper and a marker to each table. Have them write the following questions at the top of their charts:

> - Why does this team exist?
> - What is the value added by this team?
> - What are the expected outcomes?
> - What is the team's overall contribution to the system?

Ask the group to listen to your vision, including the reason for teaming. When you are finished, ask the groups to discuss the questions on the chart and make notes on the chart itself. Walk around to each group and ask if they need more information or clarification of any points you made. Allow 15-20 minutes for the groups to respond to the chart questions. While they are working, prepare four charts, each with one of the questions from the list above. For example, one chart will say, "Why does this team exist?" The second chart will say, "What is the value added by this team?" and so on. Tape them to the wall. Ask each team to share the answers they have on their charts. Compile a master list on the appropriate wall charts. Once all teams have shared, have them look at the wall charts and clear up any misconceptions about the mission.

MATERIALS YOU WILL NEED
a piece of chart paper and a magic marker per group
4 charts with the questions written on them
masking tape

The best kept secret in America today is that people would rather work harder for something they believe in than enjoy a pampered idleness. —John W. Gardner

I BELIEVE

BACKGROUND

During one of my teaming workshops I mentioned how important it is to have a team mission. A woman raised her hand and with a long face told me her team had a mission but that it didn't seem to make any difference in the quality of its work. She said the team didn't ever refer to it. During the break I asked her to tell me the story. It turned out that when three of the teachers on the team suggested they develop a clearly defined mission, the rest of the team told them to go ahead and write something. They would decide if it was O.K. The three teachers tackled the task with gusto. They finished the mission and the rest of the team said it was great. Presto...it was adopted. I must say it was well written. In fact, it was quite grand.

What happened in this situation? First, the entire team didn't have ownership. The mission was the effort of a few. Second, even though the mission was well written, it was not based on the values of the team. If the team had done a values audit and correlated their mission with their values, I guarantee they would be walking their talk. It takes commitment to go through the process but I have found when teams are willing to make that commitment it is always worth the effort.

DID YOU KNOW

- Team members characteristically exhibit a high degree of individualistic behavior due to the many different beliefs, values, and assumptions they make about the purpose of what they are doing.
- The different values and beliefs of team members often lead them to be at odds with one another.
- The team mission should be stated in writing, be clearly understood, be visible to the teams, and guide the team's actions.

Something of Value

Ask team members to pretend that they have a son or daughter who
has just accepted a first job. One day they run into an adult who
says, "Oh, you are ____'s parents. I work with him/her."

Make a list of some of the things you would like this person to say
about your son or daughter. Once they complete this list tell them to get
a piece of chart paper and draw two large circles. Label one circle SAME,
label the other circle DIFFERENT. Have a discussion about the similari-
ties and differences among team members.

Make the following points: The things they listed can be described as
values. When we have children we spend most of our parent life trying to
help our children develop these values. We often don't talk about values,
and it is possible for team members to respect each other but be at odds
due to differences in values.

Give the team a stack of 4x6 cards and some magic markers. Team
members break up into pairs. Each pair brainstorms for ten or fifteen
minutes to generate values that they hold in high esteem concerning their
work. Mention to the team that they might want to think of what their
work means in today's society, what do they value about leadership,
individual difference, community, etc. This list is not exhaustive, it just
gets them thinking.

Each pair is to write each different value on a card. Tell them they
can write one to four words on a card. When time is up each pair shares
its cards with the team. Throw out any duplicates from other pairs, and
tape the rest on the wall.

When all the values are displayed on the wall, give each person five
colored stick-on dots. Instruct everyone to move around the room and
read all the value cards. They are to vote for the values that are most
important to them by sticking a dot on a value card. Individuals may
stick all five dots on one card, or three dots on a card and two on
another, or any combination they like.

After the voting is finished, throw away any card with no sticker dots. The entire group looks at the value cards on the wall and places them in groups. For example, cards that say collaboration, shared decision making, team work, trust, and communication might be grouped together. Once this step has been completed the team names the categories. An example might be Leadership or Collegiality.

The team looks at the results and discusses what the activity revealed about the values the team members hold in high esteem. The next step is for the team to look at their values and discuss the following questions:

- Why do you value that?

- Is that view consistent with what we know about...(work, leadership, etc.)

- How does this value relate to our view on...(work, leadership, etc.)

- How does this value differ from the way we do business now?

- Is there anything we have left out?

MATERIALS YOU WILL NEED
5-6 index cards per pair
1 magic marker per pair
masking tape
5 sticker dots per person

#**22**

We're Mission Bound and Down

E xplain that a team mission statement is composed of one to four sentences that answer three questions:

- What function does the team perform?
- For whom does the team perform this function?
- How does the team go about achieving this function?

Place a chart on the wall with the statement:

WHAT FUNCTION DOES THE TEAM PERFORM?

Ask the team members to develop a list of statements that describe the function of the team. For example, a middle school might list "to discuss as a team any students having problems." A nursing staff team might list "to determine if there is a gap between care goals and what we are actually doing." An automobile quality-control team might list "to make our product more appealing to safety-conscious customers."

Once the team members complete this list, have them examine each function statement and decide for whom the function is intended. For example the function statement, "to discuss as a team any students having problems" is for the student and the teachers, so the team would write in the margin "students and teachers."

Place a chart on the wall with the statement:

WHAT DOES THE TEAM NEED TO FUNCTION?

Ask the team to develop statements that define what the team needs in order to function.

When the team members have completed the lists, they are ready to draft their mission statement. They look at their list and in a comprehensive statement of one to four sentences capture the essence of all the lists. The mission statement must not be so wordy that it is hard to understand or hard to remember.

MATERIALS YOU WILL NEED
1 chart entitled "What Function Does the Team Perform?"
1 chart entitled "What Does the Team Need to Function?"
1 chart to draft a mission statement
a magic marker

FOR
tHE
COMMITTED

Let's Get Critical

O nce the team members write their mission they may want to take it a step further and identify some critical issues. Use the following handout.

CRITICAL ISSUES

- What changes in the organization's structure are necessary for us to accomplish our team mission?
- What new capabilities and resources will we require?
- What are the implications for current beliefs, policies, and procedures?
- What are the consequences of staying with the way we are doing things now?
- What is the impact of the new way of doing things on our internal and external customers?
- How can we effectively evaluate our new way of doing things?

Lead a discussion concerning the critical issues. This discussion may take two or three team meetings. The investment in time is important because if these issues go unresolved the team may not be able to carry out its mission effectively. Write each issue discussed on a piece of chart paper and record the responses. Have the team members discuss what steps they must take to deal with the critical issues.

MATERIALS YOU WILL NEED
a piece of chart paper for each critical issue to be discussed
magic markers
masking tape

DISCOVERING
LEADERSHIP

*Have you ever met someone you would call an unforgettable character?
One time I was on an airplane and I sat next to a man who told me his
life story. He had spent seventeen years in a maximum security prison for
armed robbery. As he told his story I learned that he was "The Man" in
prison. Nothing went down without his permission...he literally ran the
show. I began to get a little nervous. I glanced down at his feet to see if
they were shackled. I just knew he was being transported covertly to
another prison. He noticed my discomfort immediately and smiled. "Are
you nervous?" he asked. I giggled like a teenager and lied, "Oh no, why
do you say that?" "You look nervous. Don't worry, I'm on the up and
up nowadays" he said. The plane landed before he finished his fascinat-
ing story. He gave me his business card, and we parted company. End of
story? No! Months later I was reading a brochure someone had given me
about an outstanding motivational speaker whose fee was $3000 per
day. I flipped the brochure over to look at the picture and lo and behold,
there was my plane mate! I was so stunned I called him up and told him
I wanted to hear "the rest of the story." He told me that while in prison,
a teacher noticed he had leadership skills. The teacher offered to get him
some help if he would accept the responsibility of leadership and use his
skills to lead a positive life. He accepted the leadership role with gusto
and the rest is history. Now he is one of the most sought-out motivational speakers in the U.S. and is considered to be a leader in the area of
organizational change.*

T his individual was willing to make the commitment to developing his leadership skills. He then accepted the responsibility of putting his skills to work in a constructive way. Warren Bennis, in his book, *Why Leaders Can't Lead* makes an important distinction between leaders of people and managers of people. He says, "Leaders are people who do the right thing; managers are people who do things right."

This chapter will help your team select a leader who will do the right thing. This can only happen if the team spends time thinking about what leadership should look like for their team to function and if they carefully select their leader or leaders. One thing about a team that makes it different from a committee is that on a team leadership can be shared. However, before the team decides to rotate leadership among the team members it needs to be sure that everyone wants to be a leader, and that everyone has leadership skills.

I often see one of three types of leadership emerge on teams. One type occurs when an administrator or other "higher-up" is on the team. In this case the team sometimes automatically chooses him or her to lead. I believe this happens because people are afraid to choose someone different. They may be afraid it would hurt the administrator's feelings or they may be afraid of retribution from the administrator. Maybe they don't believe anyone else can lead. Maybe they don't have enough trust that the administrator would be able to sit back and let someone have the role.

The second type of leadership I sometimes see is one where "anyone will do as long as it's not me." The team doesn't discuss or really evaluate the type of person they think should be their team leader. No one wants the job much less has any idea what leadership entails.

The third type of leadership I have seen is the type where one person wants the role because he or she is into status and power. When this person becomes leader, look out! He or she is the boss and shared decision making just went out the door. This person's motto is, "My way or hit the highway!" He or she often sees this as an opportunity to run the show.

When these types of leadership emerge the team will continue to function but at a very low level. In fact, one really couldn't call it a team. It becomes a committee.

Edwards Deming (1986) says it is very important to institute leadership. His attributes of leaders are:
- They understand how the team's mission fits into the overall aims of the organization.
- They try to create joy in work for everybody.

- They try to optimize the education, skills, and abilities of everyone, and help everyone to improve.
- They are coaches and counselors, not judges.
- They use the scientific process to solve problems.
- They work hard to improve the system they work in.
- The create trust.
- They do not expect perfection.
- They listen and learn.

In order for a team to function it must have strong leadership. People are energized through leadership. One of the most powerful effects of leadership is empowerment of the team members. This empowerment manifests itself in the way the team members feel about their impact on the team. Team members value learning, and competence matters. The team has a sense of community. Work becomes exciting. People look forward to the team meetings. They are motivated to work because the leader pulls instead of pushes them toward the goals.

The type of leadership I am talking about is not for the fainthearted. It is one in which the leader has clear vision, has the trust of the team, and knows and nurtures his or her own strengths. A leader helps the team do the right thing.

All resources are not obvious; great leaders find and develop available talent.—Dwight D. Eisenhower

IT TAKES TWO TO TANGO

BACKGROUND

One fine spring morning I stopped in to see one of my favorite middle school principals just to say hello. I noticed he looked kind of down in the dumps. I asked him what was wrong and he began to tell me that he was losing many of his "best" staff members to the new middle school that was opening in the fall. I tried to offer words of encouragement but secretly I thought, "Poor guy. The school won't be the same."

When I saw him again in the fall, he was smiling! I said, "Things must have changed...the teachers didn't transfer?" He looked at me and said, "Carol, it was amazing. Once those teachers left, I told the staff we were going to have to pull together and people came out of the woodwork to help organize. They are great! Who would have thought?" I was pleased for him, but what is more important, I learned a lesson. There are always people who can lead. Just find them and give them a chance.

DID YOU KNOW

- Successful leaders use all their team's strengths. They recognize, develop, and use the physical, mental, and spiritual talents of their team members.

- Building a team requires great commitment.

- A sense of humor is vital to good leadership.

SimpLE
ThiNGS
To
Do

Create a Creature

A sk the team to discuss and make a list of the characteristics of a
good leader. After they list everything they can think of, they can
use the attributes in their list to create a creature...the new leader. Label
the parts on the creature and be sure all team members can explain why
they have specific parts and what they mean in relation to leadership. For
example, the leader may have oversized ears to convey the message that
listening is an important part of leadership. Or the creature may be
dressed in a coat of many colors because he or she must deal with many
personalities. Discuss how this activity relates to helping select a team
leader.

MATERIALS YOU WILL NEED
construction paper
glue
tape
scissors
large chart paper
other materials one might use to make the creature

Simple
Things
To
Do

Leader Reflection

A sk team members to think of the best leader they have ever worked for. Have them share their story with the group. When everyone has had a turn, ask them to list attributes these leaders had that made them favorites. Have the recorder write the attributes on a large piece of chart paper. Then ask them to clarify each of the attributes and reach consensus on the five they think are the most important. The team members can then decide who among them has these qualities.

MATERIALS YOU WILL NEED
a piece of chart paper
a magic marker
masking tape

Risk

D raw a chart with three columns labeled "Looks Like," "Sounds Like," and "Feels Like." Brainstorm with the team words that describe what a leader looks and sounds like. Then list words that describe the climate he or she would create in the "Feels Like" column. In the following meetings, give every team member a chance to be the leader for one team meeting. When everyone has had a chance to try out the role, lead a discussion about which person best fits the picture they created.

Looks Like	Sounds Like	Feels Like

MATERIALS YOU WILL NEED
a piece of chart paper labeled as directed
masking tape
a magic marker

Simple
Things
To
Do

$^{\#}$27

Sold to the Highest Bidder

A sk the team to brainstorm twenty characteristics of a good leader. Have the recorder write the characteristics on a large piece of chart paper. Give each member $500 in play money. Distribute the money in different denominations. Ask for a volunteer to be the auctioneer. The auctioneer will auction off the different characteristics. Each team member buys the characteristics that he or she values most in a leader. Once everyone has spent his or her money, lead a discussion about why certain characteristics are valuable to them.

MATERIALS YOU WILL NEED
$500 worth of play money for each team member
a piece of chart paper
a magic marker
masking tape

Simple
Things
To
Do

I've Been There

Ask the team members to reflect on a time when they were in charge of something. It could be something in their personal lives such as the cake sale for a club, their child's little league team, or planning a retirement party. The experience can be negative or positive. Ask them to tell the group what they learned about leadership from their experience. When everyone has had a turn, ask team members to tell which of the shared experiences stood out for them and why.

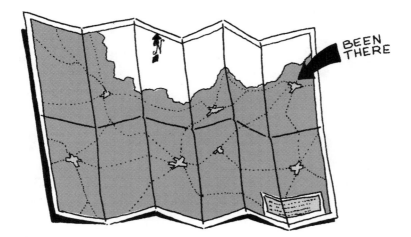

MATERIALS YOU WILL NEED

*No man will make a great leader
who wants to do it all himself, or to
get all the credit for doing it.*
—Andrew Carnegie

THE POWER OF ONE

BACKGROUND

I received a call one day from a woman who wanted me to do a motivational keynote for the entire school system. When I asked her the topic she replied that it was to be a special day for the school system in honor of all the hard work they had done that year. I talked to this woman a number of times nailing down details, etc. During one of our phone conversations I asked her what position she held in the school system. When she said, "Superintendent," I almost fell out of my chair. She was the most unassuming leader I had ever met. When I arrived she took me around to meet some of her people. The most memorable was when she passed the custodian, stopped, introduced me to him as if he were the superintendent, and then put her hand on his shoulder and asked him about his son who was being shipped out to the Gulf War. I was so impressed with her respectful treatment of the staff. She seemed to be the kind of leader who gave all the credit to others and received a kingdom in return.

DID YOU KNOW

- When learning leadership skills, it is best to start out working on a single skill, to learn that skill well, and then begin developing the other skills one at a time.
- You cannot consistently behave in a way that is different from your self-image.
- Effective leaders help team members find their own ways of getting the job done better than before.
- Effective leaders know themselves.

Things
That
Take
Effort

Big Book

A sk each team member to bring an article on leadership to the next meeting. As they share the articles, have them bring out important points. Ask the recorder to list the points on a chart. Then have the team synthesize all the articles by creating a Big Book. It is called a Big Book because the team creates a story about leadership with illustrations using chart paper and markers. Some examples I have seen are:

> Dorothy and The Wiz
>
> The Adventures of Leaderperson
>
> The Country Western Music Leadership Awards

The team writes its story around themes or ideas and interjects the main points on leadership from the articles.

When the team has finished its Big Book, lead a discussion about what they learned about leadership

MATERIALS YOU WILL NEED
several pieces of chart paper
assorted magic markers
glue
stapler and staples
scissors
construction paper

#30

Things
That
Take
Effort

Tell it Like it Is

G ive each team member a handout with the following questions on it:

- What would appeal to you about being team leader?
- What would not appeal to you about being team leader?
- How do you think a leader influences a team?
- What would be stressful about being a leader?
- Why would the team want to follow you?
- What do you think are the most important qualities a leader must have?
- Who would make a good leader for our team?

Ask them to read the questions and reflect on them until the next team meeting when they will be asked to discuss their thoughts.

At the next team meeting, put each of the questions on a separate chart. There are seven questions so there will be seven charts. Have each team member select a different color magic marker. As members individually respond to the questions, they record answers on the charts using their magic marker.

At the end of the team meeting ask them to think about everyone's responses for a week. During the next team meeting, have them discuss who on their team they want as the leader.

MATERIALS YOU WILL NEED
7 pieces of chart paper
magic markers of assorted colors
masking tape
handout with questions

Leadership means vision, cheer leading, enthusiasm, love, trust, verve, passion, obsession, consistency, creating heroes, coaching, and numerous other things.
—Tom Peters

HE'S GOT THE WHOLE WORLD IN HIS HANDS

BACKGROUND

I once knew a leader who had great vision. He had read all the books, had seen all the movies, and could quote all the quotes. He promised great things. In the day when everyone was crying the economic blues he somehow found money to finance his vision. Sounds great, doesn't it? It could have been, but as he was telling his staff how much he knew and where he was going to lead them he forgot to treat them with dignity. He started down the road to excellence but no one followed. He wasn't worried because he was the leader—he would push them. For three years he pushed, and for three years they pushed back. He no longer pushes...He was fired.

DID YOU KNOW

- Fifteen percent of the reason people get a job, keep a job, and move up in a job is due to technical skills and knowledge. Eighty-five percent of the reason people get a job, keep a job, and move up in a job is due to their people skills and people knowledge.

- Effective leaders allow and encourage regular learning and growth opportunities for the team.

- People don't care how much you know until they know how much you care.

- What team members really want is a leader whose competence and concern they can trust.

- It is the team leader who creates and maintains channels that enable the team to do its work.

- A leader cannot be imposed on a group. The leader must earn the right to lead even if he or she has been appointed.

Empower or Bust

G ive each team member a copy of *The Empowered Manager* by
Peter Block. Assign each team member a number of chapters to
read. For example, if there are ten chapters and five team members,
assign each person two chapters to read. Give them two weeks to read
and be ready to share with the entire team what they learn.

Once the team members discuss the entire book, they can discuss
what they think "empowerment" means and how it relates to leadership.
Together select a person to be the team leader who has the capacity to be
an empowered leader.

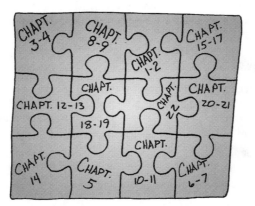

MATERIALS YOU WILL NEED
a copy of *The Empowered Manager* by Peter Block for each team
member

For
the
Committed

Who Will it Be?

After the team has met three or four times, distribute the "Leadership Functions Check Sheet" handout to each team member (see next page). Ask team members to spend the next week completing the handout and bring it back to the next team meeting.

At the next meeting, make a large mockup of the handout and record each member's responses. Lead the team in a discussion of the responses and decide who seems to be emerging as the natural team leader. Ask that person if he or she would accept the role of team leader.

MATERIALS YOU WILL NEED
1 "Leadership Functions Check Sheet" handout per team member
a magic marker
a big mockup of the "Leadership Functions Check Sheet"

LEADERSHIP FUNCTIONS CHECK SHEET

Instructions: The following are kinds of leadership behavior that usually are engaged in by someone in a group. Read each item carefully and mark a check [✓] under the phrase that most accurately describes whoever performs that function in your team.

	No One	Formal Leader	Group Members (give names if possible)
1. Who usually brings together individual contributions?	_____	_____	_____
2. Who ensures that the team makes decisions?	_____	_____	_____
3. Who begins our meetings or starts our work?	_____	_____	_____
4. Who keeps a check on whether objectives are set?	_____	_____	_____
5. Who ensures that we follow an effective method of working together?	_____	_____	_____
6. Who puts energy into the team to start us off or help us when we seem stuck?	_____	_____	_____
7. Who watches over our operation and picks us up if we omit stages of working?	_____	_____	_____
8. Who finds and brings in external information to help our work stay relevant?	_____	_____	_____
9. Who represents us as a team with other groups or teams?	_____	_____	_____
10. Who summarizes and clarifies after our discussions?	_____	_____	_____
11. Who encourages contributions from team members?	_____	_____	_____
12. Who supports other members in difficult situations?	_____	_____	_____

Reprinted from: Dave Francis and Don Young *Improving Work Groups: A Practical Manual for Team Building*, San Diego, CA: Pfeiffer & Company, 1979. Used with permission.

For
the
Committed

Do Your Homework

G ive each team member a copy of the handout "I Think a Team Leader Should…." Ask the members to complete it before the next team meeting. At the next meeting ask each member to share his or her responses and compile a master list of each of the columns. Have the team members decide if they want a single leader or if they want to rotate leadership. Give the master list to the leader(s) to use as a guide.

I THINK A TEAM LEADER SHOULD…

I think a leader should have the following abilities…	I would help the team reach its goals by…
I would build team cohesiveness by…	I would plan for the good of the group by…

MATERIALS YOU WILL NEED
1 "I Think A Team Leader Should…" handout per person
1-2 pieces of chart paper
masking tape
a magic marker

For
the
Committed

On Solid Ground

Have the team select a task or objective to complete within the hour. (Task suggestions: build a structure of straws at least four feet high, plan an overseas trip for the staff, design the government of the future.) Set up a video camera in the room to record what people say and do. Tell the group the camera is to give them feedback later. Once they start working they will forget the camera. When the task is complete, lead a team discussion about who they think emerged as the leader and why. They may have different opinions. Then play the video back and observe. Have them list all leadership traits they see. Decide who emerged as the natural leader and see if that person would like to serve as the team's first leader.

MATERIALS YOU WILL NEED
video camera
TV monitor
any materials for the task they are to complete
1 piece of chart paper
a magic marker

For
the
Committed

What's Your Concern?

Draw two large circles on chart paper. Label one circle "Concerns." Label the second circle "Influence." Have the team members list all their concerns about leadership of their team. Anything goes—don't allow anyone to make fun or negate anyone's concern. Once the circles have been filled, lead a discussion about which ones they have some direct influence over (i.e., the ones they can change). List these in the circle marked "Influence." Once they look at what they can influence, they can develop a plan of action.

MATERIALS YOU WILL NEED
2 pieces of chart paper
a magic marker
masking tape

ESTABLISHING ROLES AND RESPONSIBILITIES

I remember the first time I tried out for a play. The director handed me a script and said, "Read!" I had no idea what role I was reading. I looked up after a few minutes of reading only to see the director's lip curling into a disgusted sneer. With a wave of his hand he said, "No, no, no, nooo." He dismissed me...just like that. I was furious. I went to the back of the theater with the script and pouted for about ten minutes. All of a sudden I was struck by the fact that I had failed not because I couldn't play the part, but because no one had clearly defined my role. I didn't know what I was responsible for. I opened the script, read the role, and began to visualize myself in the part. It took me about thirty minutes to get the role and responsibilities down. I lifted my head in the air and marched down the aisle to the director. I told him that I wanted to read for the part. He looked me up and down and said, "You've already had a chance. What makes you think you could do it now?" I looked him up and down and said, "Because I now have a clearly defined picture of the role I'm supposed to play." "Humph! Oh for heaven's sake get on with it," he said. I did, and I won the role.

W hen I am in a training setting I assign roles to all the partici-pants at a table. They smile, laugh, accept the role, and then go through the training not really taking their role seriously. If team members do not take roles and responsibilities seriously, then they will end up doing what they have always done—that is, work as a committee. If a team is truly going to be effective, it must commit to doing things differently.

A team that wants to do things differently seriously considers what roles it needs for the team to function at its highest level. When the individual team members understand the roles they can better understand the jobs of all the team members. They discover how they can work together to support each other in these roles. Establishing roles helps team members understand where they fit within the team and how they contribute to the achievement of the team's mission.

Teams also need to clarify role descriptions and select the right person for the role. *Role ambiguity* results when a team member does not have a clear picture of what is expected of him or her. *Role conflict* occurs when a person cannot perform an assigned role or has a picture of what constitutes the role that is different from that of his or her teammates.

It is important for team members to be successful in their roles. They can succeed if they use their special strengths and talents, evaluate their role, check their perceptions with other team members from time to time, and deal with problems and conflicts as they occur.

This chapter is designed to help teams clearly understand the type of roles needed and to understand the expectations of the roles. Working as a team to define roles and expectations will help inspire team members to achieve commitment and success and, what is more important, to accomplish their mission.

Be yourself. Who else is better qualified?—Anonymous

TURN THIS THING AROUND

BACKGROUND
In most of my workshops I ask participants to work in teams. The participants usually have fun with the process and do a lot of laughing and kidding. On this one day I told the small groups to select the person with the largest shoe size to be the team leader. As I watched them point and heard them laugh I found myself smiling at my cleverness. All of a sudden a hand shot up for the back of the room. You know, the kind that goes up with such force it could launch a rocket...the kind you can't ignore. As I acknowledged the person she rose out of her chair and said in a loud booming voice, "I don't appreciate being called Big Foot. I suggest in the future that you use something more appropriate. You have ruined my day. Not to mention I don't like my role." I was so stunned you could have knocked me over with a feather. I must admit that when I thought about it I could see her point. I learned my lesson. I now give people a list of the roles and responsibilities and let them select the person that best fits the role.

DID YOU KNOW
- If the team is to be successful, everyone must be aware of the importance of roles.
- Everyone on the team must have a role.
- All roles are of equal importance.
- Everyone is accountable.
- When a team has problems it's often because it hasn't clearly defined the roles.

#36

Simple
Things
To
Do

Everybody's in the Act

D istribute the "Everybody's in the Act" handout (see next page). Ask a team member to read the first set of directions in the first role box to select the Facilitator. Once this person has been selected have them move to the next box until all roles have been assigned. If there are more than five people on the team the Timekeeper/Materials Specialist can be separated into two jobs. The team can decide on the duration of the roles. They may decide to change every few weeks, every month, etc.

MATERIALS YOU WILL NEED
1 "Everybody's in the Act" handout per team member

EVERYBODY'S IN THE ACT

Once you have been selected for a part you are not eligible for another role.

Casting directors are now filling the following roles. Please note how the positions will be filled.

CAST RESPONSIBILITIES

Group interaction is key.

Roles are shared.

Members share responsibility for the group.

All members are equally important.

 Count to 3. Point to a person. Whomever gets the most points becomes the **Facilitator**.

Role: *Keep group on task and make sure everyone has equal opportunity to participate.*

 Ask who has been in their field the longest. This person becomes the **Recorder**.

Role: *Record information team needs to have in order to process.*

 Look around the group and select the person who is kind, upbeat, and likes people. This is the **Encourager**.

Role: *Give the team feedback on their team behaviors and cheer the team onward and upward.*

 Select the person who likes to move around, wiggles a lot, and loves breaks. This is the **TimeKeeper/ Materials Specialist**.

Role: *Inform the team of time allotments and get all materials the team needs to perform activity.*

 The remaining person becomes the **Spokesperson**.

Role: *Represent the team's thoughts to the total group.*

Five Card Draw

P ut the roles and descriptions below on 4x6 cards. At the first team gathering ask each person to draw a card and read the role and role description. The members then discuss which roles would best suit them. Feel free to add to role descriptions.

Card I

Leader

- keep team on task
- make sure everyone participates
- lead the discussion for the next agenda

Card 2

Recorder

- record the minutes
- do chart work if necessary

Card 3

Timekeeper

- keep up with time and give ten-minute warning, five-minute warning, etc., so meeting doesn't run over allotted time

Card 4

Materials Person

- bring necessary materials to the meeting
- set up meeting space if any equipment is needed

Card 5

Observer

- collect data on teaming skills and give feedback on how the team is doing

Card 6

Encourager

- tell the team when they do something well and encourage them when they are down

Card 7

Question Captain

- make sure all questions are answered or will be answered by next meeting
- keep a list of important questions

Card 8

Checker

- check the team's perceptions of what is going on

MATERIALS YOU WILL NEED
1 set of role cards

Simple
Things
To
Do

You're Up

Bring the set of role cards listed in activity #37 ("Five Card Draw") to the team meeting. Ask each person to select a card and play that role for one team meeting. At the end of the team meeting redistribute the role cards so that everyone will have a different role for the next meeting. When everyone has had an opportunity to do all the roles have a team meeting and decide who best fits what role. If they agree to accept, they keep that role for the year or whatever time the team designates.

MATERIALS YOU WILL NEED
1 set of role cards from activity #37

Simple
Things
To
Do

Watch Where You Sit

At a team meeting, place a set of role cards (from activity #37) face down in the chairs where the team members will sit. Each person is responsible for the role that is in his or her chair for that day. Team members can always swap roles.

MATERIALS YOU WILL NEED
1 set of role cards from activity #37

Simple Things To Do

Sign on the Dotted Line

D uring a team meeting, lead the team in a brainstorming session about all the possible roles the team needs to function. As team members come up with role descriptions, have one team member write the roles and descriptions on a laminated chart. Whoever gets to the next team meeting first signs up for the role he or she would like to have for the meeting. The next person who arrives signs up for the role of his or her choice, etc. The members may trade or try to bargain for the role of their choice but they may not harass or make a team member feel bad if he or she doesn't want to trade.

Leader	*Megan*
Recorder	*Nancy*
Timekeeper	*Peter*
Encourager	*Rhonda*

MATERIALS YOU WILL NEED
a laminated chart
a magic marker

#41

Simple
Things
To
Do

Slap a Role

Have the team gather around a table while one person slowly turns the role cards (from activity #37) over. When a team member sees the role he or she wants for the day, he or she has to be the first to slap the card. If no one slaps some of the role cards just put them back in the deck and keep using them until everyone has a role.

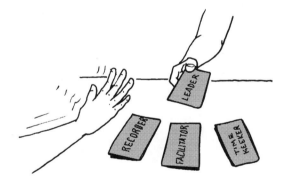

MATERIALS YOU WILL NEED
1 set of role cards from activity #37

I feel the greatest reward is the opportunity to do more.
—Jonas Salk

HIGH HOPES

BACKGROUND

Are you ever amazed that anything in this world gets done? I am! I work with thousands of smart, well-meaning people each year and yet when I observe teams working together I notice some interesting behaviors. For example, have you ever noticed in some team meetings everyone is leading? Or, even more interesting, no one is leading? I have heard team members say, "No, you do it!" Another one says, "Not me, you do it!" This goes back and forth until finally a member says, "Oh heck, I'll do it! But you're going to do it next time."

I think one of the funniest things I've heard while observing a team was the following exchange among three members.

"Did you bring the stuff?"

"What stuff?"

"Whatever someone was supposed to bring to the meeting."

"I didn't bring it. Maybe Rose brought it."

"I don't know what you're talking about."

"Oh well, no big deal. It must not have been important since we can't remember what it was or who was supposed to bring it. Maybe someone else knows."

I finally figured out that the reason these things happen has nothing to do with intelligence. It has to do with never having sat down as a team and discussed roles and responsibilities. I have learned that even a simple approach to roles and role descriptions is better than nothing. I have also learned that the more effort a team puts into this the more successful the team will be.

DID YOU KNOW

- A role is a person's place on the team—the part he or she expects to play and that others expect him or her to play.

- Defining roles and responsibilities is one of the most challenging problems a team faces.

- Once teams learn about roles and responsibilities and realize the importance of them it is fairly easy to correct problems.

- You seldom have to coerce, goad, or force team members to work in a team when they have clearly defined roles.

#**42**

Things
That
Take
Effort

My Momma Told Me Not to Brag But . . .

T his activity is designed to give the team members an opportunity to reflect on the roles that are available and that they feel they could do well. Put the following list of roles and descriptions on a chart, blackboard, or overhead:

ROLES

Team Facilitator	leads discussion, keeps people on task, helps enforce behavior norms
Leader	represents the team at other meetings, takes issues to the administration, supports the team and takes care of distributing minutes to administrator, steps in to resolve conflict if facilitator needs help
Scribe	keeps the minutes for the team meetings, reads any parts to the team that they call for, keeps a team copy and gets one ready for the leader to give to the supervisor
Observer	collects informal data concerning teaming skills and role performance in order to give the team feedback on how they are doing
Encourager	keeps the team's spirits up, helps design ways the team can celebrate their successes and learn from mistakes
Time Keeper	keeps the team aware of the time frame they have agreed to work in, gives time updates such as "ten minutes to go," etc.
Materials Person	makes sure the team has the resources they need for the meeting

Tell the team they have ten minutes to read and think about the different roles. Then go around the table and ask each person to say what role he or she would do well and why. The team decides who will have what role and for how long.

MATERIALS YOU WILL NEED
1 list of the roles and role descriptions on a chart, blackboard, or overhead

Put it in the Job Description

W rite the roles from activity #42 on a chart, blackboard, or over-head, but leave the descriptions out. Have a discussion about how the team thinks the roles should be described. Write the role descriptions based on their conversation. These become the team roles. The team can use any of the activities in this chapter to assign the roles.

Wanted: Motivated
Leader: Able to listen
effectively, to make
informed decisions,
set deadlines and
inspire a team to
success.

Wanted: Motivated
Recorder: Able to
listen effectively to

MATERIALS YOU WILL NEED
1 role list from activity #42

Things
That
Take
Effort

Take a Letter

A sk team members to write a letter to the team describing the role they want. They must list five to ten reasons why they should have the role and list three things they will do to be sure they do a good job. The team members listen to everyone then decide who gets what role.

MATERIALS YOU WILL NEED
a piece of paper and a pencil for each team member

A Team Effort

U sing the role list from activity #42, write the roles on a chart, blackboard, or overhead without the descriptions. The team may want to look at the roles listed and add or delete some. Give everyone a large sheet of paper and ask them to make a web for each role (see the illustration for web model). For example, if there are nine roles there will be nine webs, etc. Have them spend a few minutes on each role webbing words that describe what the role should entail. Next have a large web for each role on a chart at the front of the meeting room. Start with a role and ask team members for words that best describe the role. When each role has been webbed with contributions from the entire team write a role description for each one.

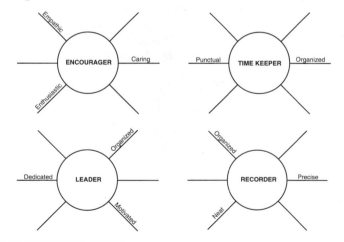

MATERIALS YOU WILL NEED
a large piece of paper and a magic marker per team member
1 piece of chart paper per role from activity #42
masking tape

Door Number One, Two, or Three?

L ist the roles and descriptions from activity #42 on a chart, blackboard, or overhead. Ask the team to discuss the roles and decide if
any should be added or deleted. Give team members a piece of paper and
ask them to list their first, second, and third preference for a role. Have
team members look at the lists and use them to distribute roles. Make an
effort to give people a role they prefer.

MATERIALS YOU WILL NEED
role list and descriptions from activity #42 on a chart, blackboard,
   or overhead
a piece of paper and a pencil for each team member

Use what talents you possess. The woods would be very silent if no birds sang there except those that sang best.—Anonymous

IF THEY COULD SEE ME NOW!

BACKGROUND

I remember a conversation I once had with Dr. Rosemary Lambie, my mentor and friend. We were talking about using people. She told me that when it came to getting people to do a job, if I used them well I would always be successful. At first I wasn't quite sure what she meant, but as I grew older and more experienced I realized that when people are doing a job they like and can do successfully you never have to ask them twice or worry about whether it will get done. I believe this holds true for teaming. If the team members take the time to think of the roles they need to have, and give them to the appropriate people, the performance level of the team will skyrocket.

DID YOU KNOW

- Well done is better than well said.
- Once the team defines and accepts its roles, it experiences a dramatic increase in cohesiveness.
- Team members must not only be responsible for their individual roles but also must support the roles of others.
- Feedback on performance is necessary to be successful in a role.
- When a team works together to define roles it helps to inspire each member's commitment.

For
tHe
Committed

Storming

Lead the team in a review of its mission statement. As people review their mission ask them to brainstorm all the possible roles they need in order to have a quality team. Once they get a list, they can write their role descriptions. They then match roles to the team members who are best qualified. They may take two or three meetings to decide who would be best for the roles. Some team members may want to try the role for a few weeks, receive feedback from the team members, and then decide if it's the best role for them. During this time suggest that the team members interview other successful teams and compare roles. They may want to add new roles they hadn't thought of or change the descriptions as they become more familiar with teaming. The key is to monitor constantly and adjust the roles to make them more efficient.

MATERIALS YOU WILL NEED
a copy of the team's mission statement
a large piece of paper
a magic marker

#48

FOR
THE
COMMITTED

Go Fishing

B efore the next team meeting, give each member six large index cards and ask them to write on each card a characteristic of themselves that they bring to the team. Ask them to write three positive characteristics and three characteristics that may not be positive. For example, a positive characteristic might be "having a sense of humor." A negative one might be "stickler about time." Have everyone share their cards and hang them on the wall. Then have them brainstorm all the roles the team needs in order to function at a quality level. Place a list of the roles on the wall. Next have them write the descriptions of the roles. Once this is done, have them look at the characteristics on the wall and determine who would be best for a specific role. For example, the person who is a stickler for time would be a great time keeper. This person would help the team abide by the time limits and at the same time would be happy because he or she would be sure that things started and ended on time.

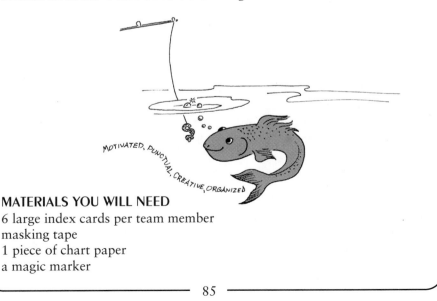

MATERIALS YOU WILL NEED
6 large index cards per team member
masking tape
1 piece of chart paper
a magic marker

For
the
Committed

You Get What You Expect

H ave the team members use one of the activities in this chapter to establish what roles they need for their team to function. After each team member has had a role for a month, give out the worksheet "What Did I Expect?" Ask each member to complete it and bring it to the next team meeting.

WHAT DID I EXPECT?

What I expected from my role	What I am discovering about my role	Support I need to do my role

At the next team meeting ask each team member to share what he or she has written on the handout column by column. After reading each column have the team member ask for comments from the group. When everyone has had a turn, ask the team members to share how this activity will help them be more successful in their role. Make a list of how they will support each other using their comments.

MATERIALS YOU WILL NEED
1 "What Did I Expect?" handout per person
a large piece of chart paper
a magic marker
masking tape

For
the
Committed

That's What I Like!

Y ou can't do this activity until the team members have their roles and have done them for a while. Every few months or so put a chart on the wall with the headings: "What I like best about my role," "What I like least about my role," "I could do my role better if...." Ask each member to respond while the recorder writes the responses in the appropriate column. The team discusses the responses as they see fit.

Now ask each team member to select a partner. Have each pair get a piece of chart paper and two markers (one color for each person). Ask them to divide the chart paper into three columns and label it as follows:

What you do well as a ___	What can I do to help you in your role as ___	An idea I had about your role is ___

Ask each person to give the other person feedback. For example, under the first column one might say and write, "What you do well as a leader is to make sure that we all treat each other with dignity. You check to see that we still understand the mission."

MATERIALS YOU WILL NEED
3 charts for the first three questions
masking tape
1 piece of chart paper per pair
2 different color magic markers per pair

For
the
Committed

Grumble, Grit, and Groan!

T his activity is a good one to do after the team members have had a role assignment for a month or so. Ask the team to stand up and begin talking simultaneously about their roles. They can complain and share reservations, resentments, gripes, or concerns. When they run out of things to grumble about, have them let out a loud groan and sit down. When you think the team has had enough time to get some of the negative energy out, call time. Then have the team focus on the following questions:

How did you feel during this exercise?

What are the benefits of this exercise?

What issues do we need to discuss?

Are we ready to move on?

MATERIALS TO BE USED
a set of questions on a chart, blackboard, or overhead

CODE OF
CONDUCT

In the early 1980s a large school district hired me to head up its staff development department. I had no sooner arrived at the central office and sat down at my desk when I heard a knock on my door. I looked up to see two of my soon-to-be best friends standing at my door. I smiled, greeted them warmly, and was just about to say something funny when I noticed they had real serious looks on their faces. I immediately wiped the smile from my face and said, "What's up?" Their eyes shifted from side to side, scoping out the area. They lowered their voices, entered the office, closed the door, and said, "We have some things we need to tell you about working here." I found myself whispering in reply, "Tell me, is it dangerous?" "No, no," they replied but there are some unwritten rules around here. If you happen to break one you will be in BIG trouble. They filled me in for the next thirty minutes. I took notes and was happily employed there for six years.

O rganizations, groups, committees, and teams will automatically develop a code of conduct. The most effective of these will be ones in which input from the employees has been solicited and agreed upon.

I define a team as a group of five to nine people who are highly energetic, work well together, respect each other, work toward common goals, and produce high-quality results. Clearly, having people skills is essential to team success.

This chapter is about team members taking responsibility for and establishing their own norms and standards. It is about holding each other accountable for excellence. Most teams do not do this step in the teaming process. They use a reactive approach rather than a proactive approach. They wait until something goes wrong to set norms for the team.

This chapter is important because it establishes the culture of the team. When I say, "culture" I mean "the way we do things around here." The culture a team wants to develop is one of inclusiveness, a feeling that everyone on the team is welcome. There is no pressure to conform. Different styles are accepted. The team members are committed to one another.

Another characteristic that the culture should strive for is realism. Teams need to look at a problem and come up with the most realistic solution, a solution not based on politics, favoritism, or any other superfluous reason. Somewhere in the code of conduct, norms need to be established so that people have permission to be heard. In this climate, if the team is going astray someone will speak up and say, "Wait a minute, I can't go along with this." An important part of realism is humility. Team members appreciate the gifts other team members have and begin to recognize their own limitations. This helps build interdependence on the team. Think about it—would you rather work with an arrogant team or a humble one?

A team needs to build a culture of contemplation. This means the team has discussed and established a number of ways to examine itself. Teams must begin self-examination right from the start. No team will automatically stay in good health. When the team needs to recover from something they focus on recovery. They will drop the current task or goal and heal themselves. This is one more major difference between a committee and a team. A committee continues on at all costs to get the task done. On a team the task and maintenance of the team are equally important.

The team culture should be one that makes the team meeting a safe place. A safe place is created through trust and team norms that foster safety. Active listening, ways to handle conflict, and, most importantly, how to treat each other with dignity should all be part of team norms. The team will need to discuss what dignity looks like, sounds like, and feels like.

A team needs a culture that can fight with dignity. There will be issues that come up that make team members examine their values. Sometimes an issue may call for rethinking some of those values, a very emotional prospect. In many instances conflict is healthy, but teams must establish norms for conflict or it can get out of hand.

A team needs to develop a spirit. The team should delight in itself and the work it does. I am not talking about a competitive spirit in which one work team thinks it is better than another work team. A true sense of spirit is one of peace. It is one where there is a strong bond of caring, a real sense of wisdom, consensual decision making, and respecful treatment of others.

When you care you win. Too many people are so involved in getting the job done or in doing what they consider their own work they forget to use common sense—which is treating other people as you know you would like to be treated.
—Donna Edton, VP,
Campbell Soup Co.

I JUST DROPPED IN TO SEE WHAT CONDITION MY CONDITION WAS IN

BACKGROUND

I have been doing team training a number of years now and never once when I ask people to tell me what they know do they ever mention setting norms for team behavior. It's as if they think it will just happen. When we get to the section on developing the team's code of conduct you would think I had given them the keys to the kingdom. They say if they had not learned anything else but code of conduct the time would have been well spent. They thank me and tell me how wise I am. Somehow I just can't bring myself to tell them I didn't discover code of conduct... someone taught me.

DID YOU KNOW

- Teams will automatically develop a code of conduct or standard operating procedure—the question is...is it effective?
- Every team should develop norms of behavior for the team to follow.
- Teams, like individuals, have short attention spans.
- Ignoring the mechanics of team work will undoubtedly lead to trouble.

Simple
Things
To
Do

Play by the Rules

A sk the group to brainstorm a list of rules that will help the team function smoothly. Write the rules on a piece of chart paper. Once the team completes the brainstorm have everyone look at the list and clarify any rules that are not clear. Then ask the group to see if some of the suggestions are the same. If so, eliminate duplicates. Next ask the team to look at the list and categorize the ideas. For example, there may be ideas on the list that have to do with how members treat each other during a discussion. That category would be called Discussion Norms. All the items that have to do with discussion go under that category. Have the team go through the entire list. Once all the categories have been made, have the team take each one and develop norms and rules. If there are seven categories there will be seven norms, and so forth. The team now has a set of norms by which they will operate. From time to time you may need to revise or add to them.

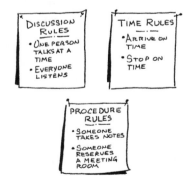

MATERIALS YOU WILL NEED
1 piece of chart paper for the brainstorm
8-10 pieces of chart paper to use for the different categories
masking tape
a magic marker

#53

Survival on Mars

Distribute a copy of the "Survival on Mars" handout to each team member. Tell them to read the directions very carefully starting with Step 1. Remind them that Steps 2 and 3 are to be done alone and Step 4 is a team effort. Ask one person to be the observer. Tell the observer that he or she is to watch the team intently and record all behaviors. For example, he or she might record that all the team members talked at once, or that one person made fun of someone's idea, or that one person didn't participate. At the end of thirty minutes stop the team. Next, the observer shares the list of observed behaviors. The team listens and then decides what kind of team rules they might need in order to work together successfully. They draft a list of norms. Once the list is drafted they have a team discussion for clarification. The norms they develop become the rules for the way the team members treat each other.

SURVIVAL ON MARS

You and your teammates have landed on Mars. The planet is inhabited by unfriendly aliens who have told you they will spare your life only if you and your team can create a successful school for their forty children of all ages. They are going to give you two days to come up with one. The curriculum is up to you. You can only send one supply list back to earth requesting ten items. What ten items would you choose to have sent?

Step 1   Decide with the team if you are going to stay on Mars and try to establish a school or if you are going to try to escape.

Step 2   Each team member makes a list of the ten items to be sent by rocket from Earth.

Step 3 Each team member rank orders his or her items from first choice to last choice with number one being the first choice, etc.

Step 4 The team members share their items and reach consensus on the top ten items they will have sent from Earth.

Note: If yours is not a school team, change the word "school" to whatever organization you are working with. For example, if your team works for a hospital, have it establish a hospital that would help the aliens become healthier. This is a versatile activity. The idea is to have an activity in which people can be observed while working together.

MATERIALS YOU WILL NEED
1 "Survival on Mars" handout per team member
a large piece of chart paper and a magic marker
a piece of paper and a pencil for each team member
masking tape

#54

Simple
Things
To
Do

How Can I Help?

L ead the team in a group discussion of behaviors that will help the
team function effectively. Have the team recorder make a list of the
suggestions on a large piece of chart paper. Ask if they need any clarification. Ask the recorder to put the following statement on a chart:

I'm good at _____ so when _____ happens I'll be responsible for
_____.

As the team members look at the behaviors listed on the chart, they
choose one they think they could do and make a statement such as, "I'm
good at staying on task so when the team has been off task over five
minutes I'll be responsible for getting them back on task by giving a
signal." Have the recorder record the responses on the chart. Each team
member should be responsible for something on the list. Some team
members may take more than one. After the team has accounted for the
entire list, it can use this chart as the norms for behavior during the team
meetings.

MATERIALS YOU WILL NEED
several pieces of chart paper
masking tape
a magic marker

Simple
Things
To
Do

Problems? What Problems?

Tell the team members they are going to have an opportunity to reflect on all the possible problems that could occur that would keep the team from functioning at its highest level. As they think of all the possible problems that could occur, they write each problem on a 4x6 card and put it in a box. Once all the cards are in, let each person pull one out, read the problem, and offer a suggestion about how to handle it. The team may add suggestions. After the team members have discussed all problems ask them to talk about how this activity relates to them and how they could use it to make them a stronger team.

MATERIALS YOU WILL NEED
3-4 4x6 index cards per team member
pencils or magic markers

#56

Simple
Things
To
Do

Metaphors or Bust

Put each of the following metaphors on a separate piece of chart paper and ask the team to complete the sentences. The recorder records the responses.

> A team that has norms is an ocean because...
>
> A team that works well together is a present because...
>
> A team that works well together is a superhighway because...

Read the metaphors and lead the team in a discussion about why they need to develop a set of norms right away, as opposed to waiting until they have met a few times. Then ask each team member to take a week to think of some norms that are important for the team to have. They are to come to the next meeting with their suggestions. At that time the team will decide which norms they will use for their team.

MATERIALS YOU WILL NEED
several pieces of chart paper
magic markers
masking tape

SIMPLE
THINGS
TO
DO

Let's Be Sensible

Put the Multi-sensory Chart on an easel or give a copy of the chart to the team.

MULTI-SENSORY CHART

Looks Like	Feels Like

Smells Like	Tastes Like

Sounds Like

Tell the team members to think about the idea of norms and rules. Ask them to come up with five words in each category that describe what rules would feel like, look like, smell like, taste like, and sound like.

When the team has completed the chart they are to make a metaphor using at least one word from each box. They may add words. Once they complete the metaphor, lead the team in a discussion about why norms and rules are essential in order to function.

MULTI-SENSORY CHART

Looks Like
- a box
- a harbor
- a line

Feels Like
- warm fuzzies
- velvet
- cozy fire

Smells Like
- perfume
- coffee brewing
- camp fire

Tastes Like
- honey
- bitter sweet chocolate
- salsa

Sounds Like
- a cheering crowd
- a symphony
- a cat purring

MATERIALS YOU WILL NEED
1 copy of the Multi-sensory Chart
1 piece of chart paper
magic markers
masking tape

Simple
Things
To
Do

Why Should We?

E xplain to the team that they are going to be discussing team norms
and rules from three different angles. Place the PCI chart on the
blackboard or on a large sheet of chart paper.

P	C	I
will add structure to our meetings	rules may be hard to enforce	we've never tried rules before
we might get more done	rules might feel artificial	if it works for debates, it might work for us

Explain that the "P" stands for *Positive*, the "C" stands for *Concerns*,
and the "I" stands for *Interesting*. Lead the team in a discussion about
some positive points about having team rules, some concerns about
having team rules, and interesting things about having team rules. Have
the recorder record the responses on the chart under the appropriate
letters. Invite the team members to set a time to select a procedure from
this book that will enable them to develop a set of norms and rules for
their team.

MATERIALS YOU WILL NEED
1 PCI chart
a magic marker
masking tape

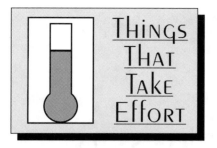

Did you ever see a committee of five work? One man does all the work; two men tell him how to do it; one man pats him on the back for doing it well; and the fifth man keeps the minutes of the meeting.
—Anonymous

PUTTING IT TOGETHER

BACKGROUND

Not long ago a school asked me to visit and observe its teams in action. My role was to observe their team members' behaviors, ask them if they needed any additional help, and find out how things were going. I visited a number of teams that day and I saw a variety of behaviors, but I'll never forget one team—the one the principal said was the best. When I arrived, they were sitting randomly throughout the classroom. One was grading papers, and one kept telling everyone to hurry up. There was no agenda. Someone just started talking. Some members were listening and some were not. Somehow they got on the topic of how they made decisions. The leader said he just did what he thought was best whenever he couldn't get everyone together. Someone said, "You do?!" It was dropped. They spent some time complaining about how things were working. They didn't decide on, or even discuss, solutions. At the end of the hour nothing had happened. The strange part of it was that they told me they really enjoyed teaming and wouldn't want to go back to the old way of doing business. You know what? I believe them. They were doing the best they knew how to do. This team had never heard of a code of conduct.

DID YOU KNOW

- Team guidelines usually prevent misunderstandings and disagreements.
- An effective and productive team does not develop by accident.
- The more individuals share in and agree on group norms the more likely they will be to like each other.
- How the team works together determines how effective it will be.
- The team should be open and flexible to new ways of doing things.

101

Things
That
Take
Effort

Absolutely Necessary

L ead the team in a discussion about what rules are absolutely
necessary in order for the team to work productively. If a team
member has a problem with any of the rules, put the Group Behavior
Problem Chart on the blackboard or a piece of chart paper and have the
team go through it. For example, a team member might say, "I have a
problem with the rule that has been suggested...only one minute per
person when discussing something. I can't go with that." You would then
take the team through the analysis so that the person with the concern
has an opportunity to share his or her feelings. You also want to be sure
that the team doesn't just throw out what may be a good norm. All that
may be needed are minor adjustments to the rule or norm.

GROUP BEHAVIOR PROBLEM CHART

1. Review information about the problem.

2. Define the behavior the team would like to have.

3. Brainstorm the options.

4. Agree and act on the team's choices.

MATERIALS YOU WILL NEED
1 chart entitled "Group Behavior Problem Chart"
a magic marker
masking tape

THiNGS
THAT
TAKE
EFFORT

I Hate It When...

A sk each team member to think of a time they worked with a group of people and got upset because of a specific behavior. Tell them to list on a piece of paper at least five behaviors that irritate them in groups. Each person shares. The recorder records the responses. Help the team to reach consensus on the top five irritating behaviors. Team members discuss the five and spend time developing norms so that these behaviors do not occur on their team.

> TOP FIVE MOST
>   IRRITATING
>   BEHAVIORS
>
> 1. EVERYONE TALKING
>   AT ONCE
> 2. TAPPING PENCILS
> 3. PRIVATE CONVERSATIONS
>   ON SIDE
> 4. PEOPLE FALLING
>   ASLEEP
> 5. UNFOCUSED
>   DISCUSSIONS

MATERIALS YOU WILL NEED
1 piece of chart paper
a magic marker
masking tape
a piece of paper and a pencil for each team member

Things
That
Take
Effort

What's Happening?

A fter the team has met four or five times, give each team member the "What's Happening?" handout. Ask them to complete it and be ready to share it at the next team meeting. At the next team meeting ask the members to share their responses. The recorder records the responses. After everyone shares, invite the team to discuss what they need to do to carry out some of the suggestions.

WHAT'S HAPPENING?

I. What three behaviors helped the team function smoothly?

2. One thing I could have done to help the team work together is...

3. One thing I think the other team members could do to help the team work together is....

MATERIALS YOU WILL NEED
1 "What's Happening?" handout per person
1 piece of chart paper
a magic marker
masking tape

#62

Things
That
Take
Effort

What's the Word?

L ead the team in a discussion about all the norms they think are necessary for the team to function. As team members come up with norms, have the recorder write them on a piece of chart paper for all to see. Once you have a list of norms you all are satisifed with, turn the team's attention to the "Norms Analysis" chart. Ask the recorder to put the first norm in the column marked "Norm." Decide together if that norm is one the team needs to work on, or if it is no problem. Put a check mark in the appropriate column and then write a comment. Do this for all the norms on your list. When you are finished, return to the norms you need to work on and devise an action plan for working on them.

NORMS ANALYSIS CHART

NORM	NEED TO WORK ON	NO PROBLEM	COMMENTS
1. Take turns speaking	✓		We interrupt each other sometimes, especially when we disagree.
2. End meetings on time		✓	We're good at time-keeping.
3. Everyone does their fair share	✓		Some people end up doing more than others because some people are busier to begin with.

MATERIALS YOU WILL NEED
1 piece of chart paper
a magic marker
1 "Norms Analysis" chart

ThiNGS
ThAT
TAke
EffoRT

Turning Wrongs Into Rights

L ead the team members in a discussion of behaviors they do not like
to see when working in a group. Keep listing the responses on a
piece of chart paper until you have about ten responses. Lead them in a
second discussion about behaviors they like to see when working in a
group. They must tell why they like these specific behaviors. Record
about ten or so of these behaviors on a second chart. On a third piece of
chart paper, they are to transform each behavior on the first list into a
behavior they would like. Have the team destroy the first list with flair
(shred it up, stomp on it, or whatever). Focus on the third list now and
discuss how they can incorporate those behaviors into their team's
functioning.

MATERIALS YOU WILL NEED
3 pieces of chart paper
magic markers
masking tape

The hardest thing to give is in.
—Anonymous

ONLY THE STRONG SURVIVE

BACKGROUND

I often use the story of General Pickett and General Grant when I talk about people working together for the good of the team. Rumor has it that one evening after a battle General Grant's men were camped on one side of a river and General Pickett's on the other. General Pickett had lost. That evening General Grant heard all kinds of singing and shouting from the other side of the river. He was perplexed. Why would defeated soldiers be celebrating? He sent his scouts to see what was going on. They returned with the news that General Pickett's wife had just given birth to a son. General Grant told his men to light fires all down the river and to shout congratulations. Even in times of great strife there are rules that men live by out of respect for each other.

DID YOU KNOW

- Teams with a code of conduct are more cohesive. The meetings are often noisy, full of personal by-play, disagreement, and even conflict but it's done within limits.
- It's important for teams to work reflectively, creatively, and productively.
- All teams have a rhythm that alternates between relaxed and freewheeling discussion and well-ordered procedures.
- Groups strongly influence the behavior of their members by setting and enforcing norms.
- Individual team member acceptance is often based on how that team member conforms to the team's norms.

Let's Do It Right

I n a team discussion, ask the team if it agrees not to go any further until it has established team norms. If so, discuss whether and how to go about researching similar organizations that have already established teams that are successful. The team could ask for time to visit and ask the teams what has made them successful. When they return to their organization they can begin to establish their norms. Make sure they have established norms for the following:

Team Meetings: time, place, room arrangement
Team Participation: procedure to make sure everyone is heard
Problem Solving: a method they will use when they have a problem
Resources: how they go about getting what they need
Conflict: how they will deal with conflict
Decisions: how they will decide what technique to use for decision making
Complaints: productive procedure for handling complaints
Team Discussion: how they will handle summarizing, moving on, etc.
Evaluation: how they will evaluate the team's progress
Celebrations: how the team will celebrate
Training: how to decide what additional training they will need

The team may choose some specific team training it will need in order to learn about problem solving and conflict management. This procedure for norm development may take one or two months. This list is not exhaustive but it is a good beginning for the committed.

MATERIALS YOU WILL NEED
The materials will depend on what the team decides to do. For example, if they decide to get additional training they will need to ask the person conducting the training what materials they will need.

MANAGING
MEETINGS

Shakespeare, in his play As You Like It, *says, "All the world's a stage, the men and women merely players." If I could rewrite this line for a modern day saga it would go, "All the world is a business meeting, the men and women merely passive, bored, frustrated players." Take today. I decided to take an hour break from the writing of this book. "Why not make some phone calls?" I said. I made ten calls. Only one person was in. Where were the rest of the people? You got it...in meetings. In fact, some of the people were going to be in meetings ALL day.*

Team members need to view their meetings as important gatherings. If people consider meetings a waste of time, then eventually apathy will set in, team members will drag in late, and attendance will drop. One of the ways to keep meetings important is to have them only when they are necessary. I once visited a team whose members were upset because their schedule included an hour and thirty minutes a day to meet. I asked them if they had brainstormed other alternatives. They looked at me with shock written all over their faces. "We can do that?" they said.

Remember, when to meet and how long to meet is the team's decision. The team I described above decided to have an hour team meeting daily and thirty minutes for individual tasks. They went away feeling happy and looking forward to their new schedule.

Are there guidelines about when to meet and when not to meet? Michael Doyle and David Straus in their book *How to Make Meetings Work* give the following guidelines:

IT'S A GOOD IDEA TO HAVE A MEETING WHEN:
- a team member wants information or advice from the team
- the team needs to solve a problem or make a decision
- there is an issue that needs to be clarified
- there is a problem that involves people from another team
- there is a problem and it is not clear what it is or who is responsible for dealing with it

IT'S NOT A GOOD IDEA TO HAVE A MEETING WHEN:
- there is inadequate data or poor preparation
- when something could be communicated better by telephone, a note, or stopping by the workstation
- the meeting is for a trivial reason
- there is too much anger and hostility in the team and they need time to cool off

We are a meeting society. That is why this chapter is important. It will give your team practicable techniques that will improve the quality of your meetings. People will come away from the team meetings feeling productive, happy, and successful. Productivity will go up. Time, our most precious resource, will not be wasted. Most importantly, the team will work constructively and productively toward its mission.

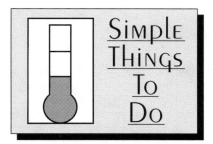

Few people know how to hold a
meeting. Even fewer know how to let
it go.—Robert Fuoss

WHAT KIND OF FOOL AM I?

BACKGROUND

I can still remember the excitement of my first year on the staff of a large
southern university. I reported to work the first day full of vim, vigor,
and enthusiasm. As I entered the outer office my heart skipped a beat as I
spied my very own mail slot...CAROL SCEARCE. As I reached into the
box I pulled out my first piece of correspondence....ATTENTION...ALL
FACULTY...MEETING 9:OO A.M. TODAY. I remember thinking I was
glad I had come in early. Gosh, what would have happened if I hadn't
checked my mail? I would have missed the meeting! As the clock struck
8:30 A.M. I pulled out my meeting announcement to see where the
meeting was to be held. "Ummm, it must be here somewhere. Oh well,
I'd better ask." I didn't want to mess up my first day. As I wandered
down the hall asking my colleagues where the meeting was, they all
responded in a very bored tone, "Who knows?" I was wild; it was
almost 9:00 a.m. I was going to be late. I began frantically looking in
every room. As I opened the sixth door I heard someone behind me. It
was my Department Chairperson. My eyes lit up; I was saved. He smiled
at me and said, "Hi, where's the meeting?"

   The next year as I entered the outer office I automatically pulled the
announcement for the first meeting out of my mailbox. As I stood there
reading, the new kid on the block walked up to me full of vim, vigor, and
enthusiasm and said, "Hi, I'm Pat! Can you tell me where we will be
meeting?" I rolled my eyes and with a bored expression responded,
"Who knows?"

DID YOU KNOW

- The results of a meeting affect the functioning of the team and its ability to achieve its objectives.
- Unnecessary meetings are time wasters; meetings should be used only when truly necessary.
- The average person will sit through more than nine thousand hours of meetings in his or her lifetime.
- Team meetings directly affect how individuals feel about their team, how committed they are to decisions, and how well they work as a team and individually.
- Many people view meetings as a necessary evil.

65

Picture This

A sk the team members to think of the best meeting they have ever attended. Give them about ten minutes to individually brainstorm and write down the reasons that meeting was successful. Pass out blank index cards. Ask them to create a visual representation or "snapshot" of the reasons on the index cards. If a team member has five reasons on his or her brainstorm list then they will have five snapshots. Have each team member explain his or her snapshots. Then glue each snapshot to a large piece of paper that represents a photo album of what a successful meeting should look like. Use this "photo album," along with an activity in this book, to develop procedures for successful meetings.

MATERIALS YOU WILL NEED
a piece of paper and a pencil for each team member
4-5 index cards for each team member
a large piece of chart paper or chart paper cut into the size of a photo
    album
glue
magic markers of assorted colors
masking tape

#66

Simple
Things
To
Do

Stand and Be Counted

Place the following statement on a chart or blackboard:

> Eyes roll, tongues wag, people sigh, a feeling of dread fills the place when a meeting of any sort is announced.

Ask the team members to discuss what the statement means, why it is or isn't an accurate portrayal of meetings, and any other thoughts they may have. Next place the following statements on a chart or a blackboard and ask everyone to respond. The recorder records the comments.

> So, why have meetings?
> Could we do without them? Why or why not?

Spend ten or fifteen minutes responding to the two questions. Then tell the team members that it is a fact that as we move toward the 21st century the vast majority of organizations couldn't function without meetings. In light of this fact, how can we be sure that our team meetings are well organized and productive? As the team discusses this, the recorder records the responses on a chart.

MATERIALS YOU WILL NEED
chart or blackboard with the quote
chart or blackboard with the questions from the activity
a magic marker
masking tape

67

Simple Things To Do

It's Been My Observation That . . .

Tell the team members that since they haven't received much training in how to hold team meetings they are going to learn from each meeting. Ask each team member to keep a team journal in which they record their thoughts and ideas about how the team meetings go and what they can do to improve them. Have the members collect this data for at least five team meetings. Devote the sixth team meeting to a team sharing of their data collection. The recorder records the ideas on a chart for future use. The team then decides the next steps it needs to take.

MATERIALS YOU WILL NEED
a notebook to be used as a journal per team member
a piece of chart paper
a magic marker
masking tape

Where I Come From
We . . .

T ell the team members that they are going to dialogue about team meetings. Explain that a dialogue and a discussion are two different things. In a dialogue, there is free and creative exploration of complex and subtle issues, a deep listening to one another, and a suspension of one's own views. In a discussion, different views are presented and defended and one view is selected.

The team members are to dialogue about what they think of meetings. What makes a meeting exciting, productive, and challenging? What makes a meeting unsuccessful?

Have the team sit in a circle with no barriers (such as a table) between members. Each team member dialogues about his or her thoughts with no interruptions, judgments, or other kinds of distracting behaviors. Each team member has an opportunity to express himself or herself. The entire team actively listens. After the dialogue, put the following chart on the blackboard or chart paper.

T-CHART

What we know	What we need to do

Lead the team in a discussion of the two questions while the recorder records the main points members make. After the discussion, the members choose the next steps they need to take to ensure that their meetings are effective.

MATERIALS YOU WILL NEED
a copy of the T-Chart
a magic marker
masking tape

Individual commitment to a group effort—that is what makes a team work, a company work, a society work, a civilization work.
—Vince Lombardi

THE GREAT PRETENDER

BACKGROUND

This story is about how I resorted to some creative insubordination to keep my sanity during unproductive meetings. I was on my way to my twentieth unproductive meeting when I ran into my friend and colleague Rosemary. She looked at me and said, "I'd rather be going anywhere than to this meeting. I have so much to do and you know this will be four hours of waste." I agreed, and off we went. As the meeting droned on my mind started to wander, and that was when the trouble began. As I looked around at all the faces my eyes stopped on an individual. All of a sudden I felt my lips involuntarily spreading into a grin. The individual looked like a penguin. I couldn't believe my eyes. I looked around the group again, and this time I saw Elmer Fudd. Next I saw an owl, and on and on.

What a menagerie. It was the funniest experience I'd had at one of these meetings. This little game was a well-kept secret. One day after a particularly boring meeting my friend Rosemary said, "Carol, at the last four meetings you seemed to be enjoying yourself. Surely you aren't enjoying the meetings?" I smiled and said, "Believe it or not, Rose, I am." She said, "How can this be? Am I missing something?" I told her she was and that if I revealed my new-found technique to her she could never tell anyone. When I told her what I was doing she looked aghast. I encouraged her to try it. She let me know that it wasn't an option, and I dropped it right there. At the next meeting we weren't twenty minutes into the agenda when the boredom set in. I began my game. My eyes caught Rosemary's. She was on the verge of slipping into craziness. I mouthed the word "owl." She quickly looked down. Five minutes later I

117

saw her staring at the owl with a smile spreading across her lips. Meetings were never boring for us again.

What is the point of this story? It took a lot of creative energy and concentrated effort to play this game. Once we learned how to play we did it with gusto. Just think of all that energy and gusto that could have been put to use had the person in charge of the meeting known how to make meetings work.

DID YOU KNOW

- The psychological reasons for meetings are: a need to feel part of a group; a need for a sense of togetherness, trust, and belonging; a need to ease the loneliness and burden of responsibility; and a need to develop a sense of commitment.

- A researcher in the area of team performance estimates that the cost of time lost due to ineffective meetings amounts to $800,000 per year for every one thousand employees.

- Most meetings are run according to some version of parliamentary procedure, which dates back to the nineteenth century.

- It's time to update how we deal with our changing environment when we get together in meetings.

- Most people have had little or no formal training in how to conduct or participate in meetings.

Things
That
Take
Effort

Preventive Medicine

A sk the team members to share what they know about having productive meetings. Have the recorder record the main points. Let the discussion go on for about ten or fifteen minutes. Write the following statements on the blackboard or chart paper for all to see:

BEFORE THE MEETING WE NEED TO:

AT THE BEGINNING OF THE MEETING WE NEED TO:

DURING THE MEETING WE NEED TO:

AT THE END OF THE MEETING WE NEED TO:

Ask the team members to suggest items or ideas under each heading that they think will help them have productive meetings. Again, the recorder records the information. Once the information has been gathered, team members discuss how and what they need to do to be sure these things get done.

MATERIALS YOU WILL NEED
several pieces of chart paper
a magic marker
masking tape

Things
That
Take
Effort

What's Up, Doc?

A sk all team members to visit another team during one of *its* meetings. They must first ask permission of the team being observed and say that they want to observe a team in action to learn about effective team meetings. The person or persons visiting are only to record things that they liked. They are to bring this information to their team and discuss how they could use this information to make their team meetings more effective.

Do not allow gossip. Gossip defeats the purpose of the visit and causes trouble within the organization.

MATERIALS YOU WILL NEED

Things
That
Take
Effort

These Are a Must

Place the following chart on the wall:

THESE ARE A MUST

AGENDAS

MINUTES

EVALUATION

Tell the team that in a productive meeting these three items have to be present. Ask the team members to work in pairs for the next two weeks researching one of these items. In other words, if two of the team members choose to work on AGENDAS, they would find sample agendas they could share with the team. They would also talk to other people who have created agendas and find out a good way to set them; read about agendas in one of the reference books listed in this book and report back; etc. After two weeks, bring the team back together and lead them in a sharing session. Have them report about all three areas. Then lead them in a discussion about how they would use this information in the most productive way. Make sure a recorder records the suggestions so team members can use them later when they develop plans for having successful meetings.

MATERIALS YOU WILL NEED
any materials the pairs collect while doing their research

Things
That
Take
Effort

Dear Teammate

Lead a discussion about what it takes to have an effective team meeting. Distribute to each team member one of the following index cards:

> Dear Teammate:
>
> Our team has a problem. At the meetings we seem to be going in different directions at the same time.

> Dear Teammate:
>
> We seem to be having a problem. Our team can never decide what topic or issue to discuss.

> Dear Teammate:
>
> I hope you can help us. We seem to have a leader who rubber-stamps all the decisions. He thinks he is being collaborative but he's not. Help!

> Dear Teammate:
>
> Our team is very vocal with a lot of ideas. Sometimes we get so many ideas we can't remember all of them. What is our problem?

Dear Teammate:

I'm going crazy. We keep going over the same old ideas again and again.

Dear Teammate:

Our team never knows from one meeting to the next what we are going to do. Why?

Dear Teammate:

I don't know how long I can attend the team meetings and not say anything. I can't hear, can't see, it's too stuffy in the room, and it's cold. Brrrrr, help me.

Dear Teammate:

Our team comes up with good suggestions but we aren't sure if we have the power to make decisions. Should we just make decisions or what?

Ask each team member to share his or her card with the rest of the team. The team discusses the possible reason or reasons for the problem and effective ways to deal with it. After members read the cards, ask if anyone would like to write a DEAR TEAMMATE card. If so, give the team a few minutes to write questions, and then ask members to share the problems and work through the same process to solve the problem. Ask the team to spend about five minutes discussing how to use this activity to make team meetings more effective.

MATERIALS YOU WILL NEED
1 set of DEAR TEAMMATE cards
extra index cards

Things
That
Take
Effort

$^{\#}$73

Can You Take the Heat?

S hare the Meetings Questionnaire with the team members. Tell them that after they have met four or five times they will complete the questionnaire. Assure them that what they write on it will remain anonymous. After the fourth or fifth meeting remind the team members to bring the questionnaire to the next meeting. Record the results on a large chart. Lead the members in a discussion about what they need to work on.

WARM — HOT

MATERIALS YOU WILL NEED
1 copy of the Meetings Questionnaire per team member
1 piece of chart paper
a magic marker
masking tape

MEETINGS QUESTIONNAIRE

Instructions: Read the three (3) scored headings and use them to evaluate each statement. Choose *one* score (4, 2, or 0) that corresponds to your opinion of how the statement applies to your meetings. Write the score in the appropriate blank.

	4 True (Usually)	2 Some- times	0 Not True (Seldom)
1. The purposes of our meetings are not defined.	_____	_____	_____
2. We do not decide what we want to achieve by the end of the meeting.	_____	_____	_____
3. People do not prepare sufficiently for our meetings.	_____	_____	_____
4. We seldom review our progress during meetings.	_____	_____	_____
5. We do not allocate meeting time well.	_____	_____	_____
6. Ideas and views often are lost or forgotten.	_____	_____	_____
7. We do not decide which agenda items have priority.	_____	_____	_____
8. We allocate equal amounts of time to trivia and important issues.	_____	_____	_____
10. People lose concentration and attention.	_____	_____	_____
11. Sometimes there are several meetings when there should be one.	_____	_____	_____
12. We do not review and confirm what has been agreed upon and how those decisions will be activated.	_____	_____	_____

Reprinted from: Dave Francis and Don Young, *Improving Work Groups: A Practical Manual for Team Building,* San Diego, CA: Pfeiffer & Company, 1979. Used with permission.

By design and by talent we were a team of specialists, and like a team of specialists in any field our performance depended both on individual excellence and on how well we worked together. None of us had to strain to understand what we had to do to complement each other's specialties; it was simply a fact, and we all tried to figure out ways to make our combination more effective.
—Bill Russell

IT MAKES ME WANT TO SHOUT!

BACKGROUND

Not long ago I was asked to spend a day and a half with thirty teams who needed help in learning how to work together. We spent much of the time learning how to design effective meetings. As I finished the training I couldn't help wondering if anything I had taught would transfer to the teachers' world of work. I didn't have long to wonder because I was invited to sit in on their first team meeting, which unbeknownst to me was that very afternoon. I crossed my fingers, held my breath, and waited.

The principal entered, gave the signal that the meeting was to begin, and started. One of the teachers raised her hand and said, "Mr. Principal, I have just been to a training session on how to have effective meetings. I would like to share some information with you and wonder if any of my colleagues would join me." The principal looked a bit shocked, but as all the other team members' hands went up he acquiesced. For the next hour they shared ideas about setting agendas, dialogue, problem solving, etc. When they finished, the administrator said, "Sounds like I should have been at that training. I tell you what: let's adjourn. No use having the meeting I planned. It's really my meeting and not a team meeting. Let's think of all the stuff we've learned and set the agenda for the next meeting. "Believe it or not, a loud cheer went up from the team. The principal won a lot of respect that day, and I believe a team was born. It made me want to shout, "It can be done, it can be done!"

DID YOU KNOW

- Meetings are an intensive way of involving others in solving problems and making decisions.

- Two questions to judge the success of a meeting are: What happened? What problems did we solve?
- Teams can learn to think reflectively, creatively, and productively.
- It is tempting to overload an agenda.
- Meetings are good for generating ideas, sharing information, and making shared decisions.

#74

FOR
THE
COMMITTED

The Meeting of the Future

Tell the team to fantasize for a moment. The year is 2000. The team has been asked to design the perfect meeting. It is the meeting that will be the model for training the rest of the organization in how to have quality meetings. Your team is to design the perfect meeting room facility, the latest in technology, ways to facilitate time for meetings, length of meetings with breaks that facilitate learning, and anything else that will ensure quality meetings.

After the team has spent thirty or forty minutes designing the meeting of the future, it comes back to reality. Ask team members to look at what they have created. Focus on what parts of their fantasy they can make come true. Lead them in developing an action plan to get what they need to have the best meetings.

MATERIALS YOU WILL NEED
chart paper
assorted magic markers
masking tape

For
the
Committed

It's Simply Got to Be There

A sk the team members to volunteer to learn about the following topics:

- problem solving
- decision making
- conflict management
- consensus
- agenda setting
- discussion methods ·
- meeting evaluation

The team members can work alone, in pairs, or in groups, as long as everyone is working on a topic. Have them spend three weeks gathering information. The bibliography in this book is an excellent resource. Other ways to learn about the topic are workshops, college classes, Human Resources Departments, other people, consultants, and audio or video tapes.

The team sets a date when everyone is to share information. Once the information is shared, the team decides on a procedure. For example, all teams need to have a problem-solving model to use. The person, pair, or group that is to bring back information on this topic may share two or three different models. The team then chooses a model that best suits it.

MATERIALS YOU WILL NEED
Whatever the person, pair, or group needs to have in order to present topic information.

GIVING AND RECEIVING FEEDBACK

When I think of giving and receiving feedback, I often think of my first years as a teacher. Once a year the administrator would come around and visit my class. He would take notes, smile sweetly, and leave. One time, I got a note in my mailbox that said, "See me!" It was like having a near-death experience. You know…your life passes in front of you. I found myself wondering if I had broken any school rules, reprimanded the wrong child, sneered at a colleague, or made a negative comment about my administrator. As I walked to the door of his office using my best placating body language I said, "You wanted to see me?" It turned out that it was conference time. Time to receive feedback on my ability to teach. It started out with a lot of "goods" and a few "greats," but as the clock ticked on I heard the dreaded word "however." I braced myself for what I knew was coming. "Carol," he said, "you need to do better on classroom management. Also, you might want to work on … ." The words became a blur. I felt like a failure. I did not hear another word. I just nodded passively while he did all the talking. I remember getting up, smiling my best fake smile, and thanking him for all his help. I went back to my room and continued to teach the way I had always taught.

Was I uncommitted, uncaring, and insubordinate? No. I wanted to be a good teacher, but in those days we didn't really know a lot about teaching or giving feedback. I am proud to say that great strides have been made in my profession in regard to giving and receiving feedback. As a result, I no longer teach as I did during my first few years.

E dwards Deming says that organizations should institute on-the-job training and vigorous programs of education and self-improvement for everyone. What better way to do this than through team feedback on performance? A team should have a system that gives each team member an opportunity to reflect on himself or herself first privately and then to the team. It should also provide feedback about whether or not the team is sticking to its mission and about how the team is abiding by its norms. This feedback should be given daily, monthly, or yearly depending on the team's needs. Every time feedback is given, an action plan should be developed that outlines what the team needs to do to perform at a higher level. The team should strive for continued growth and development.

The outcomes of team feedback on performance should be:

1. CREATING AND MANAGING TRUST

2. FACILITATING LEARNING

3. DEVELOPING AUTONOMY

Each of these goals is explained as follows:

1. CREATING AND MANAGING TRUST: Trust must be established before true feedback can be given or received. If trust has not been established the team members will "nice" each other to death: they will not tell the truth, and they will make excuses for why someone may have acted a certain way or why a task did not get done. The team must work hard to move beyond this stage in order for real growth to occur. Trust is a complex concept: it is being able to rely on the team. It is believing that team members have your best interest at heart and that their words and opinions are reliable. It is believing the team will act in a fair way when it comes to feedback. It is knowing the team has integrity.

2. FACILITATING LEARNING: As a result of the feedback process team members should learn something about themselves, about each other, and about the team as a whole. The process should be one that gives the members hope that they can get better through professional growth and development. They should find themselves thinking differently than when they first started together.

3. DEVELOPING AUTONOMY: A team that has reached this level is one that does not need much help from the outside. It has reached a high level of self-awareness, self-evaluation, and self-modifiability. Members of such a team are aware of their behaviors and the impact of

the behaviors on fellow team members. They can analyze, evaluate, and modify their team behaviors as well as design their own prescriptions for growth. They are in a continuous state of growth and are excited about where they are going.

This chapter is important because it is through feedback on performance that the team is able to reach the performing stage. The ideas in this chapter are best carried out by an assigned observer on the team.

A smile in giving honest criticism can make the difference between resentment and reform.
—Phillip Steinmetz

I REALLY DON'T WANT TO KNOW

BACKGROUND

I have no idea if the story you are about to read is true. I believe it is because I cannot imagine a teacher telling it about herself just to be funny. The story goes like this. One day a teacher was teaching a lesson. As she turned from the board, she noticed a young man with his hand in the air. She called on him. He said, "Mrs. Lee, do you like what you do?" "Yes, I like what I do!" said Mrs. Lee and went on teaching. About halfway through the lesson the young man raised his hand again. "Yes, son, what is it?" said Mrs. Lee. "Are you sure you like what you do?" asked the young man. Mrs. Lee responded, "I told you yes, now do not interrupt the lesson again." "Are you sure?" said the young man. The teacher placed her hands on her hips and with a stern look said, "For the last time, YES, I like what I do." The young man looked sheepishly at the teacher and said, "Then why don't you tell your face?" The teacher told me that in all her years of teaching she had never received feedback that affected her so profoundly.

DID YOU KNOW

- An individual can increase learning tremendously when he or she receives feedback.
- All human beings have blind spots that can limit their potential.
- The most helpful kind of feedback is very specific.
- Comments must be honest, but the dignity of the individual receiving them should have top consideration.

Reflective Questions

The first step in this activity is for you to decide if you want the team to receive and give feedback concerning one of the following areas:
- team roles
- individual performance as a team member
- the team's functioning as a whole

Once you choose the area, look at the questions listed below and rewrite them accordingly.
- What was it you expected to do?
- What do you think you did well?
- What would you do differently?
- What support do you need from the team?

For example, if the team is going to discuss team roles or team member behavior, the questions can stay as is, but if the team is going to discuss the team as a whole, you need to reword the questions as follows:
- What were we expected to do?
- What have we done well?
- What should we do differently?
- What support do we need to continue or change our performance?

Write the questions on a chart and hang them on a wall. Tell the members which of the three areas they are going to focus on for the meeting. Give the members ten minutes of silence to think of their responses. Once the time limit is up, take one question at a time and ask each team member to respond. Record the responses. Summarize the responses for each question and thank team members for being open and honest. Remind them how important feedback is to the growth of the team.

MATERIALS YOU WILL NEED
1 copy of the questions listed in the activity
1 piece of chart paper
masking tape

#77

Simple
Things
To
Do

PCI

Place the following chart on the wall.

PCI

Positive	Concern	Interesting
I always ask questions when I don't understand something.	I don't know if I'm doing a good job because no one ever tells me.	I like to take notes at meetings, but I don't know if I should share them with other people.

Lead the team members in a discussion about what they have accomplished as a team that is positive, what they have concerns about, and what has happened or not happened that is interesting. The recorder records the responses under the appropriate column.

You can use this chart as an individual feedback tool. The observer asks each individual to fill out a copy of the PCI chart. Members are to reflect on what they think they have done for the team that is POSITIVE, what about their individual performance is a CONCERN, and what they have found INTERESTING about themselves as they have worked on becoming a team member. Each team member shares his or her responses with the team. Again, this is a tool that is open to many creative adaptations.

MATERIALS YOU WILL NEED
a large PCI chart
1 copy of the PCI chart per person
a magic marker

Simple
Things
To
Do

Temperature Check

P lace the "Temperature Check" chart on the wall. Tell each team member that this is a quick way to check on the team's climate. Explain each of the categories on the chart. Then model one or two responses a team member might make. For example, a team member might select the heading APPRECIATIONS and say, "I would like to tell the team members how much I appreciate the fact they allowed me to disagree with dignity." Another team member might select PUZZLES and say, "I still do not understand how we are going to have time to do the project we said we were going to do. Could someone help me out in five seconds or less?" Someone else might say, "I have a complaint. We were really off task today. I'd like to offer my services in giving a high-five sign when we have been on task for five minutes or more." Another member might say, "I want to share a wish. I wish we could snap our fingers and make some of the barriers we are facing go away."

When everyone has had at least one opportunity to respond, thank the team and close the meeting.

MATERIALS YOU WILL NEED
1 large "Temperature Check" chart
masking tape

TEMPERATURE CHECK

APPRECIATIONS
Something you appreciate about the group, an individual, or a group process.

COMPLAINTS
Something that bothers you. Offer an alternative.

PUZZLES
Something you are confused about.

HOPES, WISHES
Something you hope or wish for concerning the team or its mission.

Simple
Things
To
Do

Support Me

Ask each person to think of how he or she could become a better team member. Ask everyone to set one or two goals for growth in relation to being a good team member and write these goals on the handout. In two months or so ask the members to bring their goal sheets to the meeting. Each team member shares his or her goals with the team and asks for support. After four months the team members revisit their goals and ask the group for feedback on how they are doing. If they need help, the group brainstorms ways to support them. For example, one team member may be quiet and want to speak up more. If this is not happening over a period of weeks, the team may think of ways to be sure the person has an opportunity to speak up.

GOALS I'VE SET FOR MYSELF

Name:_____

Goal 1

Goal 2

MATERIALS YOU WILL NEED
goal sheets

Criticism should not be querulous and wasting, but guiding, instructive, and inspiring.
—Ralph Waldo Emerson

THE FIRST CUT IS THE DEEPEST

BACKGROUND

In the early 1980s I was working for a very large school district that wanted to do a massive staff development training. Since we had three thousand teachers we decided that we would train a team of four people at each school to deliver the training on designated staff development days. I spent months training the trainers. They were like my children. I was so proud of their hard work. One point I kept stressing was that a good trainer always asks for feedback, responds to the feedback, and makes adjustments when possible.

The day arrived for the trainers to begin training others. All of us were full of fear, excitement, and high hopes. The training ended at 3:00 p.m. At 3:15 p.m. I heard a knock on my office door. Four of my trainers were standing with feedback sheets in their hands and big tears in their eyes. "Read these, read these!" they cried. As I began reading I could not understand what they could be crying about. The feedback comments were great. But as I neared the bottom of the pile my face fell. I read the following comments:

> The trainers were an insult.
> Too much time on rear could use more time on pot.
> This sucks.
> One of our trainers can't speak correct English.
> Who's the stupid that punched the holes wrong in my handouts.

I must say I was stunned that any professional would write such unkind and unprofessional comments on a feedback sheet to his or her colleagues. I wondered what these people would do to a student if he or she dared do the same to them. I would say they'd be in major trouble... wouldn't you?

141

DID YOU KNOW

- Criticism is most effective when it sounds like praise.
- It is more effective not to find fault; find a remedy.
- In order for feedback to be effective there must be a basic trust in one another.
- Feedback should not be judgmental.
- Feedback must not be interpretative.

#80

Liked/Didn't Like

Place the following chart on the wall:

THINGS I LIKED	THINGS I DIDN'T LIKE	SUGGESTIONS

Remind the team members that when they are giving this type of feedback it is imperative to treat situations and people with dignity. The feedback must be specific and not a "shame and blame game." Each team member responds using specific examples. Under the column "Things I Didn't Like," the person has to make a suggestion about how to make the situation better. For example, a team member might say, "I didn't like the fact that we were off task twenty minutes of our meeting. My suggestion is that we open our awareness level and see if this happens at our next meeting. If it does, we may want to review our roles to see who should be keeping us on task, talk about why it is not happening, and discuss how we can help this person keep us on task. Or, we may discover that the person is trying to keep us on task and we're not responding. We might want to look at why and how we can prevent this from becoming a habit."

Each team member has an opportunity to respond to any of the columns. A person can pass but has to say why. The recorder records the responses.

When everyone has had a turn the team members look at what they liked, turn to the chapter in this book on "Celebrations," and celebrate. They look at the things they didn't like and discuss and plan what they can do to prevent these things from happening.

MATERIALS YOU WILL NEED
1 large "Liked/Didn't Like" chart
a magic marker
masking tape

THiNGs
THat
TAke
Effort

How Productive Were We?

D istribute copies of the "How Productive Were We?" feedback sheet and ask each member to fill one out. The recorder records the team responses, using a large mockup of the feedback sheet. The team then discusses areas it needs to work on. This type of activity may be helpful to evaluate the team's work together at the end of a project.

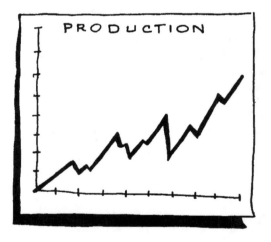

MATERIALS YOU WILL NEED
1 large "How Productive Were We?" chart and 1 copy for each team member
a magic marker
masking tape

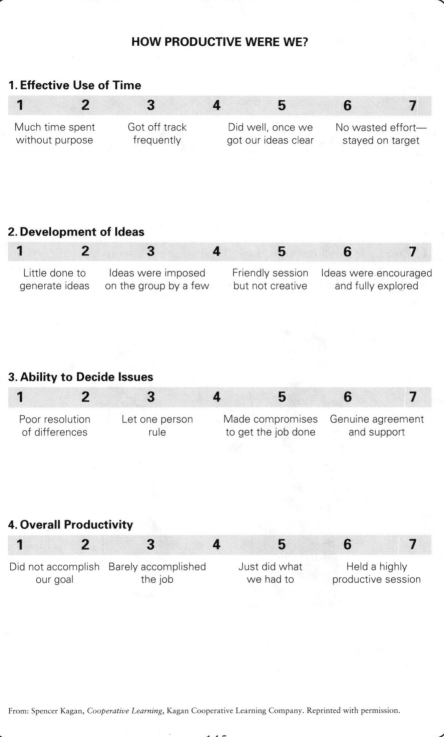

HOW PRODUCTIVE WERE WE?

1. Effective Use of Time

| 1 | 2 | 3 | 4 | 5 | 6 | 7 |

Much time spent without purpose

Got off track frequently

Did well, once we got our ideas clear

No wasted effort— stayed on target

2. Development of Ideas

| 1 | 2 | 3 | 4 | 5 | 6 | 7 |

Little done to generate ideas

Ideas were imposed on the group by a few

Friendly session but not creative

Ideas were encouraged and fully explored

3. Ability to Decide Issues

| 1 | 2 | 3 | 4 | 5 | 6 | 7 |

Poor resolution of differences

Let one person rule

Made compromises to get the job done

Genuine agreement and support

4. Overall Productivity

| 1 | 2 | 3 | 4 | 5 | 6 | 7 |

Did not accomplish our goal

Barely accomplished the job

Just did what we had to

Held a highly productive session

From: Spencer Kagan, *Cooperative Learning*, Kagan Cooperative Learning Company. Reprinted with permission.

Things
That
Take
Effort

How Helpful Was I?

Distribute copies of the "How Helpful Was I?" sheet and ask each member to fill one out. Have the team share its responses and discuss what items it needs to work on. Have members discuss what kind of help they might get from the team, and ask for feedback from the team.

MATERIALS YOU WILL NEED
1 "How Helpful Was I?" sheet per team member

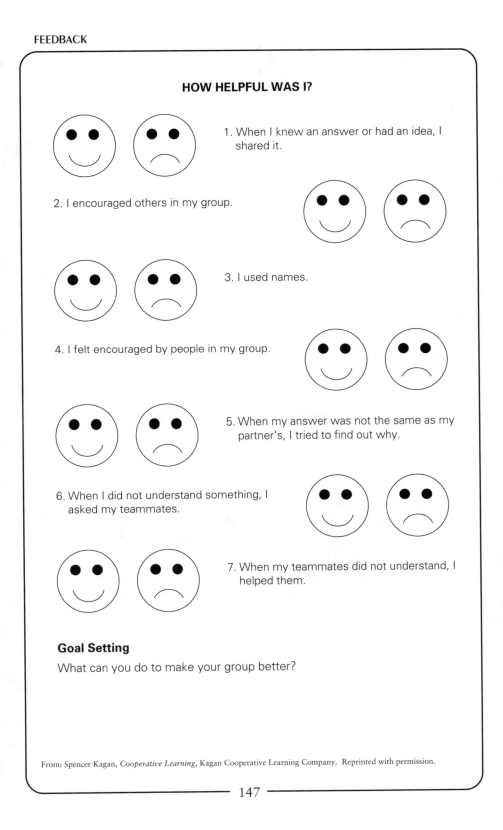

HOW HELPFUL WAS I?

1. When I knew an answer or had an idea, I shared it.

2. I encouraged others in my group.

3. I used names.

4. I felt encouraged by people in my group.

5. When my answer was not the same as my partner's, I tried to find out why.

6. When I did not understand something, I asked my teammates.

7. When my teammates did not understand, I helped them.

Goal Setting

What can you do to make your group better?

Things
That
Take
Effort

It's a Reflection

Distribute copies of the "Reflection" sheet and ask each team member to complete one. The recorder collects the sheets and records the responses on a large mockup of the sheet. The team members discuss what they need to work on and develop an action plan.

MATERIALS YOU WILL NEED
1 "Reflection" sheet per team member
1 large mockup of "Reflection" sheet
a magic marker
masking tape

REFLECTION

Use This Scale

1 Strongly Agree
2 Agree
3 Somewhat Agree
4 Disagree
5 Strongly Disagree

Name _____

Team Name _____

Date _____

Circle the Number

My Team

Agree	1	2	3	4	5	Disagree	1) Had clear goals
Agree	1	2	3	4	5	Disagree	2) Made progress toward the goals
Agree	1	2	3	4	5	Disagree	3) Stayed on task
Agree	1	2	3	4	5	Disagree	4) Made decisions based on views of all

My Teammates

Agree	1	2	3	4	5	Disagree	1) Listened well to each other
Agree	1	2	3	4	5	Disagree	2) Helped each other by giving useful suggestions
Agree	1	2	3	4	5	Disagree	3) Were respectful of all points of view
Agree	1	2	3	4	5	Disagree	4) All participated

My Suggestions for Improvement

Adapted from: Spencer Kagan, *Cooperative Learning*, Kagan Cooperative Learning Company. Reprinted with permission.

Things
That
Take
Effort

How Are We Doing?

The "How Are We Doing?" feedback sheet should be completed after the team has met four or five times. Distribute the sheet and ask the team members to reflect on the team over the past few meetings. Once team members have completed the sheets, the team recorder tallies the responses and gives the team feedback. Lead members in a discussion about what they have learned about themselves and the team. Then have them discuss what they need to work on and what they will do to improve.

𝍷𝍷𝍷𝍷𝍷 𝍷𝍷

𝍷𝍷𝍷𝍷𝍷 𝍷𝍷𝍷𝍷𝍷 𝍷𝍷

𝍷𝍷𝍷

𝍷𝍷𝍷𝍷𝍷 𝍷𝍷

𝍷𝍷𝍷𝍷

MATERIALS YOU WILL NEED
1 "How Are We Doing?" sheet per team member

HOW ARE WE DOING?

1. **What one word would you use to describe how the team was today?**

2. **What one word would describe the way you would like the team to be?**

3. **Is everyone participating?**

   Yes, always_____ Usually_____ Occasionally_____ Rarely_____ No, never_____

   If not, why not?_____

4. **Are you (everyone on team) trying to make each other feel good?**

   Yes, always_____ Usually_____ Occasionally_____ Rarely_____ No, never_____

5. **Are you trying to help each other feel able to talk and say what you think?**

   Yes, always_____ Usually_____ Occasionally_____ Rarely_____ No, never_____

6. **Are you listening to each other?**

   Yes, always_____ Usually_____ Occasionally_____ Rarely_____ No, never_____

7. **Are you showing you are listening by nodding at each other?**

   Yes, always_____ Usually_____ Occasionally_____ Rarely_____ No, never_____

8. **Are you saying "That's good" to each other when you like something?**

   Yes, always_____ Usually_____ Occasionally_____ Rarely_____ No, never_____

9. **Are you asking each other questions?**

   Yes, always_____ Usually_____ Occasionally_____ Rarely_____ No, never_____

10. **Are you listening and really trying to answer these questions?**

    Yes, always_____ Usually_____ Occasionally_____ Rarely_____ No, never_____

11. **Are you paying attention to each other?**

    Yes, always_____ Usually_____ Occasionally_____ Rarely_____ No, never_____

12. **Is there any one person talking most of the time?**

    Yes _____ No _____

Adapted from: Spencer Kagan, *Cooperative Learning*, Kagan Cooperative Learning Company. Reprinted with permission.

No one so thoroughly appreciates the value of constructive criticism as the person who gives it. —V.R. Benner

I'M ON THE OUTSIDE LOOKING IN

BACKGROUND

In order for any organization or team to grow, it needs time for reflection, autonomy, and collaboration with others. Many teams find themselves in situations in which these three factors are almost impossible to attain. Coaches have known about these factors for years. What coach would not have his or her team reflect on the previous game? What coach does not reserve the right to choose what he or she thinks are the best plays for the game? What coach does not preach collaboration on the field? What coach does not give immediate feedback on performance? I suggest it would be unconscionable not to take any of these options from a coach. Why then do we think we can become a winning team without conducting business as coaches do?

DID YOU KNOW

- Feedback helps the learner by correcting his or her own subjective perception.
- Feedback increases awareness and understanding of the team process.
- Each of us sees the world through our own autobiography. We assume our perceptions are true. Feedback helps us see a different perspective.
- We must be aware of each team member's sensitivity level or threshold for receiving feedback.
- Feedback should not come before members have a fairly clear picture of each other.
- When giving feedback, each team member must report only for himself or herself.

153

For
tHe
Committed

Portrait of Myself

Ask the team members to keep a log of their behaviors within the team, their feelings, what they think they have contributed to the team, and what they need to work on. They keep the logs for four or five meetings. Remind them to bring their logs to the sixth meeting, which will be devoted to the sharing of the reflections. Each team member reflects on one issue at a time, going around the team. Each team member asks the other members to give him or her feedback on the reality of his or her perceptions.

MATERIALS YOU WILL NEED
logs

It's Conference Time

A sk each team member to select a partner to be his or her coach. Have people tell their coaches what behaviors to observe over a two- to four-week period. These behaviors include: self-reflection, ability to work alone, and teamwork. They decide together how the coach will collect the data. Once the data is collected, the partners have a conference. Ask the coaches to talk as little as possible and let their partners talk because the person who talks the most learns the most. The coach may want to refer to activity #72 ("Dear Teammate") and use the self-assessment questions.

MATERIALS YOU WILL NEED
whatever is necessary to collect data

Let's Get Social

H ave the team observer collect data using the sociogram sheet in
this activity. The directions are on the sheet. The observer does
not participate in the team meeting when he or she is collecting the data.
Ask the observer not to share the information with the team. Two weeks
later, ask the observer to do another sociogram. After the second
sociogram, have the observer share the data from both sociograms with
the team. Have the team members discuss any patterns they see: who
participated the most and the least, and any other relevant information
they can glean from the data. They then make recommendations that
will help the team achieve equity in participation levels.

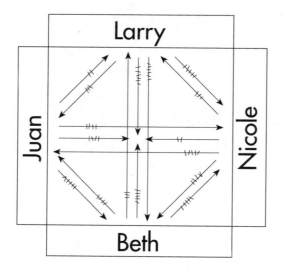

MATERIALS YOU WILL NEED
2 sociogram sheets

THE SOCIOGRAM

Instructions: The figure below represents a table. Enter the names of team members along the sides of the square, corresponding to where they sit during the meeting. When someone speaks, draw an arrow from the speaker to the person addressed by the remark. Use a slash mark across that arrow each time the pattern is repeated. If the recipient answers the remark, draw a separate arrow from this person (who is now the speaker) to the first person (who is now being addressed). If a remark is to no one in particular, draw the arrow from the speaker to the center of the square.

Hopes and Concerns

G ive team members copies of the "Hopes and Concerns" sheet during the first team meeting. Tell them to complete the sheets over the next two weeks and to bring the completed sheets to the following meeting. In that meeting, lead the team members in a discussion about how they are doing in light of what they wrote on their sheets.

HOPES AND CONCERNS

Instructions: Jot down your hopes and concerns for this project. You will probably be asked to share your answers with your teammates.

- What are your hopes for this project?
  - What do you personally want to achieve or experience?
  - What do you hope the team accomplishes?

- What are your concerns about this project?

- What are your concerns about this team?

MATERIALS YOU WILL NEED
1 "Hopes and Concerns" sheet per team member

#89

For
the
Committed

Did I Help?

G ive each team member three "Did I Help?" sheets and ask them to complete one after each team meeting for three weeks. At the end of three weeks each team member evaluates his or her performance and shares his or her responses with the team. The team can give additional feedback to the individual team members.

MATERIALS YOU WILL NEED
3 copies of the "Did I Help?"sheet per team member

DID I HELP?

Name____________________ **Group Name**________________________

Date____________________

	Often	Sometimes	Never
1. I checked to make sure everyone understood what I did.	☐	☐	☐
2. I answered any questions that were asked.	☐	☐	☐
3. I gave explanations whenever I could.	☐	☐	☐
4. I asked specific questions about what I didn't understand.	☐	☐	☐
5. When I had difficulty, I got extra practice or help.	☐	☐	☐
6. I paraphrased what others said to be sure I understood.	☐	☐	☐

How can I be more helpful?

From: Spencer Kagan, *Cooperative Learning*, Kagan Cooperative Learning Company. Reprinted with permission.

90

Recipe for a Successful Team

E very three months distribute the feedback sheet entitled "Recipe for a Successful Team." Ask the team members to complete the sheet and bring it to the next team meeting. Devote the entire team meeting to discussing the results. Have the recorder record the results. Let the team decide if it needs additional training, a change of roles, outside support, etc.

MATERIALS YOU WILL NEED
1 "Recipe for a Successful Team" sheet per team member

RECIPE FOR A SUCCESSFUL TEAM

Instructions: Read the statements and circle a number to indicate how well each describes your team. Be sure to complete both sides of the page.

		Strongly Agree			Strongly Disagree
1.	We agree on our mission.	1	2	3	4
2.	We see the mission as workable.	1	2	3	4
3.	We have a clear vision and can progress steadily toward our goals.	1	2	3	4
4.	We are clear about project goals.	1	2	3	4
5.	We are clear about the purpose of individual steps, meetings, discussions, and decisions.	1	2	3	4
6.	We have an improvement plan.	1	2	3	4
7.	We have a flowchart describing the project steps.	1	2	3	4
8.	We refer to our planning documents when discussing what direction to take next.	1	2	3	4
9.	We know what resources and training are needed throughout our project.	1	2	3	4
10.	We have formally assigned roles.	1	2	3	4
11.	We understand which roles belong to one person and which are shared, and how shared roles are switched.	1	2	3	4
12.	We use each member's talents and involve everyone in team activities.	1	2	3	4
13.	Team members speak with clarity and directness.	1	2	3	4
14.	Team members listen actively.	1	2	3	4
15.	Team members avoid interrupting and talking when others are speaking.	1	2	3	4
16.	Each team member initiates discussion.	1	2	3	4
17.	Each team member seeks information and opinions.	1	2	3	4
18.	Each team member suggests procedures for reaching goals.	1	2	3	4
19.	Each team member clarifies, summarizes, or elaborates on ideas.	1	2	3	4

		Strongly Agree			Strongly Disagree
20. Each team member acts as a gatekeeper.		1	2	3	4
21. Each team member compromises and is creative in resolving differences.		1	2	3	4
22. Each team member praises and corrects others with equal fairness.		1	2	3	4
23. We discuss how decisions will be made.		1	2	3	4
24. We explore important issues by polling.		1	2	3	4
25. We decide important issues by consensus.		1	2	3	4
26. We use data as the basis for our decisions.		1	2	3	4
27. We have reasonably balanced participation.		1	2	3	4
28. We have open discussions regarding ground rules.		1	2	3	4
29. We openly state or acknowledge norms.		1	2	3	4
30. We are sensitive to nonverbal communication.		1	2	3	4
31. We comment and intervene to correct group process problems.		1	2	3	4
32. We contribute equally to group process and meeting content.		1	2	3	4
33. We demand to see data before making decisions and question anyone who tries to act on hunches alone.		1	2	3	4
34. We use basic statistical tools to investigate problems and to gather and analyze data.		1	2	3	4
35. We dig for root causes of problems.		1	2	3	4
36. We seek permanent solutions rather than rely on quick fixes.		1	2	3	4

CELEBRATING
SUCCESSES

In April of this year I received a call from an organization that wanted me to do a motivational speech for them. They were celebrating last year's production rate. Their quality defect was zero, they had employed twenty-five new workers, and their next year's projections were the highest ever. The Chamber of Commerce had named them Outstanding Business of the Year. I told them, "No problem, I will look forward to it." I marked August on my calendar and went about my business.

In early August the CEO called and said there had been a slight modification to the plan. The small celebration had turned into a major event. The entire town wanted to join in. There was going to be a parade through town with floats, costumes, the works. The parade would culminate at the high school stadium, where the mayor and others would give their speeches. I was to be the last act. I would do my motivational speech from the football field to thousands.

Believe me, I was not pleased. In fact, I was in a panic. I found it hard to believe people would enjoy a three-hour event in hundred-degree weather. I was no longer looking forward to the engagement.

The day arrived. I drove an hour and a half to this small southern town. As I drove into the parking lot I was surprised. Not only were there floats, there were hot air balloons, concession stands, and thousands milling around with excited faces. As we all assembled, hundreds and hundreds of balloons were sent up to the loud cheers of the public. The mayor and others spoke briefly. They finished...it was now my turn to end the celebration on a high.

I closed my eyes and saw myself as my favorite rock star, Tina Turner. I took a deep breath, shot out of my chair, grabbed the microphone, and began to perform. I twisted, I turned, I told moving stories, I made some powerful points. As I moved into the final act, I gave it all I had. With my last thought, I raised my hands and said, "Celebrate, Celebrate!" I didn't get to finish the last line because a deafening roar filled my ears as the crowd rose with thunderous applause and loud cheers.

The day was a success. As I drove home, I reflected on the celebration. Why had it been such a success? I decided that these people had something important to celebrate: their successes. They were willing to take a risk...they dared to be different. Most importantly, they knew their hard efforts would pay off. Everyone was invited to the celebration and made to feel important.

Effective teams know there are many tools for inspiring individuals. They are sure to have a healthy blend of extrinsic and intrinsic rewards. Celebrations are designed around team members' belongingness needs, esteem needs, and self-actualization needs. This opens the door to an unlimited array of celebrations. Some team members respond to celebrations where there is food: some respond to applause or any type of recognition. Some only need a compliment to keep them going. The key to all of this is for team members to know each other well and to develop celebrations that are really celebrations and not feeble attempts to do something for the sake of doing something.

Effective teams know how to make celebrations happen. They have spent team time talking about what they think is important to celebrate. The team members do not compete against each other. The only comparison they make is to themselves. They celebrate regularly and promptly. They do not recognize and celebrate inferior performance.

This chapter focuses on many different types of celebrations. It is included in the book because if teaming is the vehicle your organization is going to use to transform itself, it must be a vehicle that is in good working order. One way to keep it in working order is to recognize achievement so that the team will concentrate on images of itself succeeding. Success seems to have a profound effect on performance.

It's not the lofty sails but the unseen wind that moves the ship.
—W. MacNeile Dixor

CELEBRATION... COME ON!

BACKGROUND

A few years ago I received a call from the superintendent of a small county in North Carolina. He wanted to do something special for his entire staff to celebrate all the hard work its members had done to improve their school system. I suggested the theme "School Should Be the Best Party in Town." I left it in his hands.

When I arrived to do the keynote I was stunned. For a moment I thought I had stepped into Mardi Gras. The school was decorated to the hilt. Balloons were everywhere. The tables were decorated with confetti, party bags, and hand-painted signs. You name it, it was there. The superintendent was so excited. He handed me the letter he had sent to all the teachers. It told them to sleep in until 9:00 a.m., at which time they were to join the superintendent and school board for a celebration.

We began the morning of celebration with a band whose musicians were teachers. The superintendent asked us all to stand up and join him in a dance. He made a short speech about all their accomplishments and how proud they should be. The next thing I knew five hundred people were on their feet as the superintendent said, "Let's begin this new year by sliding into excellence." With that the band started playing "The Electric Slide" and we all began to dance, the superintendent in the lead. As we laughed our way through the dance each school came forward and did a cheer, each one better than the next. The enthusiasm was so powerful I began to cry. I know that sounds silly, but I was so touched by the sincere pride the superintendent felt toward his staff.

The rest of the day is another story that's better than this one, but I think I have made my point. Celebrations are important. They send the message that people are important. They uplift spirits and create a feeling of oneness. They boost morale. People laugh and share the accomplishment of common goals. Celebrations can be wonderful culminations of successful team work.

DID YOU KNOW

- Celebration serves as an important vehicle for informal communication and mingling across groups.
- Celebration provides opportunities for employees to develop a spirit of "oneness."
- Celebration communicates a message that the organization cares about employees.
- People want to know their work matters.

Simple
Things
To
Do

Things We Have/Haven't Done

You can do this activity every month or two. Get a large piece of paper and make three columns. The first column is entitled "Great things we have done as a team!" The second column is entitled "Things we have done we <u>never</u> want to do again!" The third column is entitled "Things we haven't done that we want to do!" Ask the team members to brainstorm points under each column. When they are finished, decide together how they are going to celebrate column one.

Great things we have done as a team!	Things we have done we <u>never</u> want to do again!	Things we haven't done that we want to do!

MATERIALS YOU WILL NEED
1 large chart with the three columns mentioned in this activity
a magic marker
masking tape

Quick and Easy

Here are some ideas for celebrating at the end of each team meeting.

Silent Cheer or Arctic Shiver—Ask someone to share something the team has done well at the end of the meeting. All team members raise their hands above their heads and shake them in a silent cheer.

Standing O—Ask each team member to stand and share one good thing that happened during the team meeting. After each member has shared, tell everyone to make an O with their hands. Then say, "You have just received your first standing ovation for a job well done."

Body Signs—Ask each person to share one good thing that happened at the team meeting. After each has shared, ask the team to come up with a body sign that represents the good things shared. An example might be a thumbs-up or high-five sign.

Back Rub—Share two or three things that made the meeting successful. Then ask all the team members to stand in a line facing to the right. Each member places his or her hands on the shoulders of the person ahead, and, on the count of three, massages that person's shoulders. After a minute members turn and face the opposite direction and massage again.

Other possible celebrations include: round of applause, air guitar, and the wave.

MATERIALS YOU WILL NEED
none

From: Kay Burke, *What to Do with the Kid Who. . .: Developing Cooperation, Self-Discipline, and Responsiblity in the Classroom*, Palatine, IL: IRI/Skylight Publishing, Inc., © 1992. Reprinted with permission.

Graffiti Board

Designate a graffiti chart or board for the team. During the last five minutes of the meeting, encourage everyone to go to the board and write a word or a message that describes something the team did well during the meeting. Leave the comments up for the next couple of meetings.

MATERIALS YOU WILL NEED
graffiti board
assorted magic markers

Simple
Things
To
Do

Let's Party

O nce every two months invite another team to join you for an after-work, thirty-minute celebration party. Ask each team to share five or ten things that have happened in their team meetings that call for a celebration.

MATERIALS YOU WILL NEED
refreshments or any other materials as desired

Simple
Things
To
Do

Teammate of the Month

The team sets up criteria for this honor. At the last meeting of each month the team votes on the teammate of the month. The teammate of the month award is one free lunch, one free favor, or whatever the team decides is an appropriate reward.

MATERIALS YOU WILL NEED
whatever the team decides the award should be

The greatest humiliation in life is to work hard on something from which you expect great appreciation, and then fail to get it.
—Edgar Watson Howe

YOU'RE MY SOUL AND MY INSPIRATION

BACKGROUND

One time I worked with a team that had a really big and stressful project to do. We worked day and night. The project required a lot of cross-departmental cooperation, and we worked for months with no let-up. Tempers were starting to fray, fatigue was setting in, we began to wonder if we would ever get the project completed.

One day while sitting in my office it suddenly dawned on me that we were getting too wrapped up in the project. We were no longer having fun! I picked up the phone and called all the team members. I told them I was declaring Friday a "Swap, Buy, and Sell" day. All the members were to meet in my office. They were to bring something from home they would like to swap or trade. We were going to have some fun. At first almost everyone was reluctant. After all, we were going to take work time to play. Somehow I persuaded them to do it anyway.

Friday arrived. We all met in my office. All the members laid out their items and the "Swap, Buy, and Sell" began. It was absolutely hilarious. The funniest part was when individuals felt they had to give a sales pitch for why someone should buy their articles. We laughed until tears rolled down our faces. When the last item was gone we closed our party with each person telling one thing about the project that he or she wanted to swap, buy, or sell to another teammate. Again, this brought much laughter. Needless to say, we worked toward the completion of the project with renewed vigor and enthusiasm. My old teammates still talk about "Swap, Buy, and Sell."

175

DID YOU KNOW

- Play and fun in the workplace bonds people together, reduces conflict, and creates new visions.
- Without expressive events, any team will die.
- In a strong team nothing is too trivial to celebrate.
- A team must celebrate if it's going to thrive.
- Celebrate the inches because they lead to the touchdown.

96

Sing a Song

H ave the team develop an ad, cheer, song, or story that celebrates its successes. Have the members present their creation at a staff meeting or to other teams.

MATERIALS YOU WILL NEED
the ad, cheer, song, or story from each team
refreshments if appropriate

Things
That
Take
Effort

Spotlight Team of the Month

E ach month, put a team in the spotlight. Ask the team members to have a team picture taken and put it on a bulletin board. Have them list what their accomplishments are. Give them reserved parking spaces near the building for the month. If the team meets every week, give the members a "meeting-off" pass to use once during the month.

THIS MONTH'S TEAM

ACCOMPLISHMENTS:
1. PRODUCTIVITY INCREASE OF 13%
2. REMAKES REDUCED BY 7%

MATERIALS YOU WILL NEED
team picture
reserved sign
team "meeting-off" pass

Things
That
Take
Effort

Top Performance

A sk the entire organization to help develop some top performance awards. There is no limit to how many can be given out. If a team meets the criteria, it gets the award. If all the teams meet the criteria, all the teams are rewarded. Using the guidelines below, develop criteria and share them with the staff:

1. Determine what important things about teaming need to be rewarded.

2. Sell the program. The staff must believe in the recognition program and see that it is administered fairly.

3. Emphasize that this is not a competition or popularity contest.

4. Be careful when establishing criteria for award winners. The criteria must be as objective as possible.

5. Recognize winners regularly and promptly.

6. Do not recognize inferior performance. If there is no winner in a particular category, then don't give the award.

MATERIALS YOU WILL NEED
whatever you and the teams decide will make good awards

Don't be afraid to give your best to what semingly are small jobs. Every time you conquer one it makes you that much stronger. If you do little jobs well, the big ones tend to take care of themselves.
—Dale Carnegie

TWIST AND SHOUT!

BACKGROUND

I once attended a conference that was the best conference experience of my life. When I arrived, I received a color-coded name tag on a string to wear around my neck. The colors represented the number of years a participant had attended the conference, and everyone was required to wear the neck tag all week. The upperclassmen were in charge of taking care of the lowerclassmen. On Wednesday night there was a talent show in which participants were highly encouraged to participate. The last day of the conference was graduation, and the conference planners made a big deal out of it. When a name was called out people cheered and celebrated. Everyone I have met who has participated in this type of conference loves it. Why? Because it models what the research says about rituals and celebrations. The leaders know the impact these things have on people. Every year people return because they feel a sense of specialness—a sense of being valued as a person.

DID YOU KNOW

- Achievement deserves recognition.
- Recognition motivates higher accomplishments.
- The best-run organizations always make sure everyone understands why someone gets a reward.
- People have a way of becoming what you encourage them to be.
- Success stories have a significant ability to motivate people.
- When we see others succeed, it gives us hope that we can do it too.
- Most people are starved for appreciation.

The Best Award Ever

This activity will take two to three hours to complete. It is only for the committed.

1. Ask the team members to talk about ceremonies they have seen or heard about that they thought were great. This sets the stage. It gets team members' creative juices flowing.

2. Distribute a stack of index cards to the team members and ask them to brainstorm as many types of awards and ceremonies as they can.

3. Have each member mark his or her two best ideas for a team award. Then go around the circle and ask each person to share his or her first choice. Tape each card on the wall. Next have the members share their second choices. Then ask them to look at the rest of their cards and add any others they think should be included.

4. Have the team look at all the cards on the wall and remove any duplicates. Next, the recorder selects the first card on the list and asks the group if any of the other cards could go with this card. For example, if the first card was "Food," any card that had to do with food would go under this card. What you are doing here is grouping similar items.

5. Have each of the team members select a partner. Each pair takes one of the categories and writes a few sentences that pull all the information on the cards together. For example, if the category is "Food" and the cards under it are _luncheon_, _cocktail party_, and _a free lunch_, one might write, "One of the awards we are considering involves food such as a free lunch, a cocktail party, or a team luncheon." Once this has been done, the partners develop a pro-and-con list for this type of award.

After each category has been developed with pros and cons, the team meets to share the data. Each pair of partners shares its information with the team. After everyone has presented, the team decides which awards would be appropriate for their team.

6. The next step is to develop an action plan that includes criteria for the award, planning for the development of the award, evaluation of the

award, and anything else the team deems necessary to make the ceremony a success.

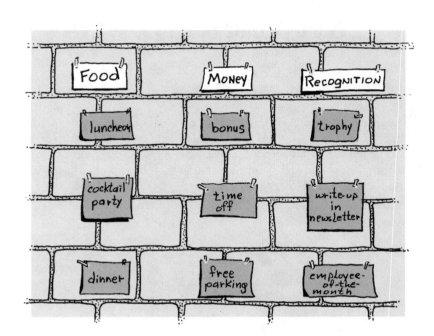

MATERIALS YOU WILL NEED
100 4x6 index cards
assorted magic markers
masking tape
chart paper

FOR
tHE
COMMItted

Everyone's Involved

The entire organization may want to plan an awards ceremony for all the teams. If so, ask each team to select one team member to represent his or her team. This team member will serve on the award development team. Use the process outlined in activity #99 and plan the awards ceremony for the entire organization.

MATERIALS YOU WILL NEED
100 4x6 index cards
assorted magic markers
masking tape
chart paper
awards of the team's choice

RESISTERS YOU WILL SEE

O rganizations are full of all types of people. Some are team players and some are not. Some are happy and some are not. Some people like activities and some do not. This section of the book is to introduce you to some of the people you will meet and to offer a suggestion or two that will help make the activities a success.

•   •   •

"I DON'T PLAY GAMES"

These people are in every group. You will recognize them by their comments and body language. You will hear them comment under their breath (loud enough for you to hear), "I can't believe we are going to cut and paste. I don't have time for this." They have their arms crossed and a frown on their face.

The best way to deal with this is to take a proactive approach. At the beginning of the training, tell your audience that active participation is a very powerful way of learning. Tell them that all the activities require thinking and doing. Let them know that this is serious but at the same time fun. Invite them to participate. If you have some people who still resist, just leave them alone. I have learned that force never works. Everyone is accountable. Your job is to know the activity, use the best learning techniques you know, and put individuals in charge of their own learning. Most importantly, do not allow yourself to be intimidated.

"I'M AN INTROVERT"

At least a fourth of your audience will be introverted. People who are introverted would rather do things alone. They get their energy from within. At times people annoy them. You will recognize the introverts because often they will enter the room and sit by themselves. If they can't sit alone they will find other introverts. They get irritated when people talk when they are supposed to be working. When called upon, they may say, "Could you give me a minute to think?"

The best way to deal with introverts is to understand them. They are great people. They like to reflect and will do some of the best thinking in the group if they are allowed to. Since you know you will have introverts, plan ahead. During the training allow think time. Give people one- or two-minute warnings before you call time. Allow enough time to complete the activity. You might state at the beginning of the training that active participation is required and that you will provide reflection time.

• • •

"I'M UNCOMMITTED"

These people are often in the training because someone told them they had to attend. I have conducted workshops in which individuals had no idea why they were there. It's hard to be committed when you don't know why you are there! The uncommitted are easy to spot. They sit in the back, and often they will let out little bark-like laughs when you give them directions for activities. They might try to intimidate you by staring a hole through you or wearing a smirk. The most intimidating are the ones who read the newspaper or clip their nails while you are talking.

My first suggestion is to breathe deeply and keep going. The most important thing is to know there will be one or two in the audience and to plan for them. When you open the session, be sure to give reasons why the training is important. The hope is that you can touch on something that will help them see what is in it for them. If that does not work, talk to them during a break. Find out something about them. Use them as examples. You might say, "Fred told me he is a math teacher. Let me give an example of how this can help math teachers." If none of this works, just ignore the person. This is hard to do, but as long as he or she is not bothering anyone it may be the only thing you can do.

"I KNOW IT ALL"

Every group has a know-it-all or two. There are two types. One type is the individual who thinks he or she knows everything there is to know about the topic. You will recognize these people because they will constantly interrupt you, they will talk when you're talking, or they will try their best to do the training for you. Then there are the types who have done this specific topic before. They have heard someone talking about the topic in the past, or they have read a book, or they went to a thirty-minute workshop and feel they don't need to know more or hear it again.

It is important for you to know which type of know-it-all a person is because the techniques for dealing with the situation are different. If you find you have the first type you must get on top of it quickly. First, acknowledge know-it-alls and thank them for sharing. After the third interruption, tell them you appreciate their knowledge and you will talk to them at the break. If that doesn't work tell them you are trying to stick to a schedule and that perhaps they would like to help you with a follow-up session. Maybe they could reproduce some of their knowledge and give it to the group. When you see their hands go up don't feel compelled to call on them. If nothing seems to work see them at a break and ask them nicely not to interrupt. This takes some nerve, but these people are persistent and they'll get over it.

If you have the second type of know-it-all, one of the best techniques is to tell the group at the beginning that you realize there are all levels of knowledge in the room. Some people will hear something and say, "I know that!" Tell those people that perhaps they could be thinking of different ways to use the information in their lives. Also tell them that if they have information that is important and that you haven't mentioned, you would appreciate their sharing it with the group. You might also tell them that often we have to hear information a couple of times before it becomes powerful or useful. Another technique is to give lots of examples of how to use the information. The main point is to help this type of person see the information in another light.

•   •   •

"I'M PASSIVE"

Bruce Joyce, in his work on different types of learners, says that a large portion of an audience is passive. By that he means that these individuals are swayed by the people around them. They have enough energy to wonder about possibilities but do not get actively involved in pursuing options. You will recognize them because they don't ever seem to get excited. They may be stallers who are hesitant, neutral, and indecisive. Worse yet, they can be unresponsive, noncommittal, and evasive. You may be doing your most rousing part of the training and look out and see a passive learner with a deadpan look on his or her face. All of a sudden your confidence begins to ebb.

These people are not harmful. They have no hidden agenda. They just don't get excited. Your best approach is to see if you can change the seating and get them next to someone who does get excited. A technique I have used is to tell the group to move around. Ask everyone to sit next to someone they haven't had an opportunity to talk to. It doesn't always work, but it is worth a try. It is also important for you to help the passive member see how the training relates to him or her. Above all, don't become discouraged, keep a positive outlook, and be sure you have a high energy level for what you are doing.

•   •   •

"WHAT'S IN THIS FOR ME?"

These people enter the room with a glint in their eye and the question, "So...now what?" forming on their lips. They have that "show me" attitude.

One suggestion for dealing with this type of person is to be sure you state the purpose of the training up front. You might even say, "Let me tell you what is in this training for you." It will be important for you to get them to participate and contribute ideas. Expand on the benefits of the training.

•   •   •

"I'M HERE TO BE SEEN"

These people are in a class all by themselves—and class is uppermost in their minds. They want to impress others, to "look good" in someone else's eyes. You'll recognize them because they will sit up front and volunteer for everything. They will be involved, but it may be at a low level. In other words they will do the activities but they may not be involved at a high level. They may be the ones who finish within five minutes. You know in your heart they could not possibly have learned what you wanted them to learn.

These people are not hard to work with because all you have to do is let them be seen and heard. Call on them, let them lead the group for a while, and talk to them on breaks. Notice them!

$$\bullet \quad \bullet \quad \bullet$$

"I'M A LIFELONG LEARNER"

I've left the best for last. We wish everyone could be like these people. They are there to learn. They are excited about the activities. They are thinking ahead to how they can use the information in their lives. They will take any and every opportunity to learn or refine an existing skill. You'll recognize them because they will sit up front with a smile on their face and even yell "Right on!" during the training. They will want copies of everything you have.

The best way to appeal to these people is to be sure you are interesting, well organized, and on-target. Then say a little prayer of thanks that these people are in your training because they make whatever other people you have to deal with worth it.

As I said earlier, some people are team players and some are not. Some like activities and some do not. The good news is that most people are absolutely delightful. I have found that when you treat people with dignity they will do any activity you ask them to do, because people in organizations want to make a difference. That's what teaming is all about.

FINAL NOTE

L ike many others who have put their thoughts on paper, I have come to realize that there are stages to writing a book. These stages apply to any creative effort, including building teams. (I have borrowed the terminology from my business and industry friends. The characteristics under each are my own.)

The first stage is **Uninformed Optimism.** It is characterized by the following thoughts:

"I know I can do it!"

"I have 1,001 ideas."

"I have something of value."

"I can't wait to begin."

"This is going to be easy."

It doesn't take long to get through this stage. After the first week the truth sets in and you immediately move into the second stage, **Informed Pessimism.** The reality of your commitment compared to your talents hits you in the face. This stage is characterized by the following thoughts:

"I don't think I have any original ideas."

"I can't do it."

"What if I fail?"

"Maybe I'll hide out in a foreign country."

The amount of time you spend in this stage depends upon your inner strength and your belief in effort versus luck. I stayed in this stage off and on for a month or so. Then with much effort I moved to stage three, **Hopeful Realism.** This stage is characterized by the following thoughts:

"Calm yourself...You can do it!"

"Oh, why not develop a plan?"

"Take some small steps. It's the inches that count!"

"Look at how much you have done. Go for it!"

This stage is what I call **the Light at the End of the Tunnel.** You know you will make it even if it takes months. It does! As you pass from this stage into the last stage, called Successful Completion, you begin to get excited as you send your last rewrite to the publisher or your team accomplishes its first goal. You breathe a sigh of relief and find this stage characterized by the following thoughts:

"It wasn't so hard."

"I did it, I did it!"

"I've forgotten the pain. I can't even remember I was ever afraid."

"I could do this forever."

As this stage draws to a close you turn your thoughts to the future... what's next?

BIBLIOGRAPHY

Atkinson, P. (1990). *Creating culture change: The key to successful total quality management*. San Diego, CA: Pfeiffer and Company.

Bellanca, J., & Fogarty, R. (1991). *Blueprints for thinking in the cooperative classroom*. Palatine, IL: IRI/Skylight Publishing, Inc.

Bennis, W. (1989). *Why leaders can't lead: The unconscious conspiracy continues*. San Francisco: Jossey-Bass.

Block, P. (1987). *The empowered manager. Positive political skills at work*. San Francisco: Jossey-Bass.

Bormann, E., & Bormann, N. (1988). *Effective small group communication: Strategies and skills*. Edina, MN: Burgess Publishing.

Burke, K. (1992). *What to do with the kid who. . .: Developing cooperation, self-discipline, and responsibility in the classroom*. Palatine, IL: IRI/Skylight Publishing, Inc.

Costa, A., & Garmston, R. (1986). *The art of cognitive coaching: Supervision for intelligent teaching*. Sacramento, CA: The Institiute for Intelligent Behavior.

Covey, S. (1989). *The 7 habits of highly effective people*. New York: Simon & Schuster Sound Ideas.

Deal, T., & Kennedy, A. (1982). *Corporate cultures: The rites and rituals of corporate life*. Reading, MA: Addison-Wesley.

Deming, W. E. (1986). *Out of crisis*. Cambridge, MA: Massachusetts Institute of Technology Center for Advanced Engineering Study.

Deming, W. E. (1986). *The Deming management method*. New York: Putnam.

Doyle, M., & Straus, D. (1976). *How to make meetings work: The new interaction method*. New York: Wyden Books.

Francis, D. & Yound, D. (1979). *Improving work groups*. San Diego, CA: University Associates.

Garfield, C. (1986). *Peak performers: The new heroes of American business*. New York: William Morrow.

Hickman, C., & Silva, M. (1984). *Creating excellence: Managing corporate culture, strategy, and change in the new age*. New York: New American Library.

Hunter, M. (1976). *Improved instruction*. El Segundo, CA: Tip Publications.

Jacobs, E., Harvill, R., & Masson, R. (1988). *Group counseling*. Pacific Grove, CA: Brooks/Cole Publishing Company

Johnson, D. & Johnson, R. (1989). *Leading the cooperative school*. Edina, MN: Interaction Book Company.

Kagan, S. (1992). *Cooperative learning*. San Juan Capistrano, CA: Resources for Teachers, Inc.

Kolb, D., Rubin, I., & McIntrye, J. (1979). *Organizational psychology: An experiential approach*. Englewood Cliffs, NJ: Prentice-Hall.

Lazear, D. (1991). *Seven ways of knowing*. Palatine, IL: IRI/Skylight Publishing, Inc.

Maddux, R. (1988). *Team building: An excercise in leadership*. Los Altos, CA: Crisp Publications.

McGinnis, A. (1985). *Bringing out the best in people*. Minneapolis, MN: Augsburg Publishing House.

Parker, G. (1990). *Team players and teamwork: The new competitive business strategy*. San Francisco: Jossey-Bass.

Peck, S. (1987). *The different drum*. New York: Simon & Schuster.

Phillips, S., & Elledge, R. (1989). *The team-building source book*. San Diego, CA: University Associates, Inc.

Quinlivan-Hall, D., & Renner, P. (1990). *In search of solutions*. Vancouver, B.C.: Training Associates, Ltd.

Schltes, P. (1988). *The team handbook*. Madison, WI: Joiner Associates.

Senge, P. (1990). *The fifth discipline: The art and practice of the learning organization*. New York: Doubleday.

Varney, G. (1989). *Building productive teams: An action guide and resource book*. San Francisco: Jossey-Bass.

Vogt, J., & Murrell, K. (1990). *Empowerment in organizations: How to spark exceptional performance*. San Diego, CA: Pfeiffer and Company.

Williams, R. B. (1993). *More than 50 ways to build team consensus*. Palatine, IL: IRI/Skylight Publishing, Inc.

Ziglar, Z. (1986). *Top performance*. Old Tappan, NJ: F. H. Revell.

NOTES

NOTES

NOTES

NOTES

Learn from Our Books *and* from Our Authors!

Bring Our Author/Trainers to Your District

At IRI/Skylight, we have assembled a unique team of outstanding author/trainers with international reputations for quality work. Each has designed high-impact programs that translate powerful new research into successful learning strategies for every student. We design each program to fit your school's or district's special needs.

1 Training Programs

Gain practical techniques and strategies for implementing the latest findings from educational research. IRI/Skylight is recognized around the world for its commitment to translating cognitive and cooperative learning research into high-quality resource materials and effective classroom practices. In each program IRI/Skylight designs, participants learn by doing the thinking and cooperating they will be asking their students to do. With IRI/Skylight's specially prepared materials, participants learn how to teach their students to learn for a lifetime.

2 Networks for Systemic Change

Through partnerships with Phi Delta Kappa and others, IRI offers two Networks for site-based systemic change: *The Network of Mindful Schools* and *The Multiple Intelligences School Network.* The Networks are designed to promote systemic school change as practical and possible when starting with a renewed vision that centers on *what* and *how* each student learns.

3 Training of Trainers

The Training of Trainers programs train your best teachers, those who provide the highest quality instruction, to coach other teachers. This not only increases the number of teachers you can afford to train in each program, but also increases the amount of coaching and follow-up that each teacher can receive from a resident expert. Our Training of Trainers programs will help you make a systemic improvement in your staff development program.

To receive a free copy of the IRI/Skylight catalog, find out more about the Networks for Systemic Change, or receive more information about trainings offered through IRI/Skylight, contact

IRI/Skylight Training and Publishing, Inc.
200 E. Wood St., Suite 274, Palatine, IL 60067
800-348-4474
FAX 847-991-6420

There are
one-story intellects,
two-story intellects, and three-story
intellects with skylights. All fact collectors, who
have no aim beyond their facts, are one-story men. Two-story men
compare, reason, generalize, using the labors of the fact collectors as
well as their own. Three-story men idealize, imagine,
predict—their best illumination comes from
above, through the skylight.
—*Oliver Wendell*
Holmes